GLOBAL RECESSION - CAUSES, IMPACTS AND REMEDIES

FINANCIAL CRISIS IN THE GLOBAL BUBBLE ECONOMY

GLOBAL RECESSION - CAUSES, IMPACTS AND REMEDIES

Additional books in this series can be found on Nova's website under the Series tab.

Additional E-books in this series can be found on Nova's website under the E-books tab.

GLOBAL RECESSION - CAUSES, IMPACTS AND REMEDIES

FINANCIAL CRISIS IN THE GLOBAL BUBBLE ECONOMY

AKINORI TOMOHARA
AND
MOLLY SHERLOCK
EDITORS

Nova Science Publishers, Inc.
New York

For permission to use material from this book please contact us:
Telephone 631-231-7269; Fax 631-231-8175
Web Site: http://www.novapublishers.com

Additional color graphics may be available in the e-book version of this book.

Library of Congress Cataloging-in-Publication Data

Financial crisis in the global bubble economy / editors, Akinori Tomohara, Molly Sherlock.
p. cm.
Includes index.
ISBN 978-1-61740-597-0 (softcover)
1. United States--Economic conditions--2001-2009. 2. Financial crises--United States. 3. Housing--Prices--United States. 4. Business cycles. 5. Banks and banking. I. Tomohara, Akinori. II. Sherlock, Molly F.

HC106.83.F54 2010
330.973'0931--dc22

2010013751

Published by Nova Science Publishers, Inc. † New York

CONTENTS

PREFACE

The current financial crisis is the most severe economic crisis that most of today's practicing economists and students of economics have personally experienced. It is expected that the United States economy will recover slowly, and that a full recovery will take many months, or even years. The 3rd quarter of 2009 showed strongly positive growth in national gross domestic product, indicating that a recovery may be underway. Additionally, there is evidence of a turn-around in housing markets, the collapse of which was a significant contributor to the United States economic woes. However, not all indicators suggest that the United States is in for a robust recovery. As of October 2009, unemployment was still increasing, surpassing 10 percent nationwide. Further, large budget deficits and an accelerating national debt have begun to generate concern regarding a future path of economic stability. High rates of unemployment and record levels of national debt indicate that there are significant macroeconomic concerns and that policymakers must remain vigilant in their efforts to restore macroeconomic stability and stable economic growth.

As the United States economy enters a period of recovery, this book assembles new research providing insight regarding the type of policies that may be effective in expediting recovery and preventing recessionary relapse. A review of the ongoing financial crisis in the United States provides background information and context for this discussion. Present concerns about stock market bubbles emphasize the importance of understanding factors impacting stock prices during financial crises. Research here examines the impact of corporate governance structures on stock prices in Japan during the recent economic crisis. The bubble in the housing market was a major factor contributing to economic and financial crisis in the United States. Possible causes for and evidence on the status of the U.S. housing bubble is presented as well. Research in this volume also addresses the spread of financial crises across countries, or contagion. Understanding contagion is important in an increasingly globalizing economy. As sovereign economies experience increasing international linkages on a number of economic, financial, and trade related dimensions, it is important to understand the risks associated with such relationships.

This volume is intended for a broad audience of academics, policymakers, and students. While some chapters employ more advanced mathematical and technical analysis, key macroeconomic insights and implications are intuitively explained throughout the text, making the policy conclusions accessible to those less familiar with some of the technical methodologies. The current economic crisis has raised many questions regarding the applicability of modern macroeconomic theory and approaches to real world problems. This text provides macroeconomic insight into the current economic crisis, simultaneously addressing policy options for recovery that will contribute to reshaping the understanding of macroeconomic crises and recovery.

The contributors to this volume are experts in economics drawing from a variety of academic and policy experiences providing unique perspectives into financial crises. The following paragraphs briefly highlight the key elements of each of the five chapters in this volume.

The first chapter of this text provides an overview of the financial crisis focusing on the experience of the United States. The financial crisis in the United States was characterized by a collapse of the housing market, a severe credit crunch, and extreme instability in the broader financial sector. There were severe and lasting consequences for the real economy, as observed via stagnation in economic growth, high rates of unemployment, and losses in wealth. Policymakers in the United States responded aggressively using expansionary monetary and fiscal policy tools. Macroeconomic indicators suggest that these policies may have been effective in pushing the United States toward the path of recovery.

The second chapter examines the recent Japanese financial crisis by focusing on Japanese stock returns in late 2007 and 2008. Specifically, the chapter examines the impact of corporate governance structures on stock prices. The findings suggest that Japanese firms' adoption of a stock option plan and the level of non-Japanese shareholders are negatively related to a stock's performance. The findings in this chapter suggest that during a financial crisis corporate governance structures are related to the overall performance of a firm.

The third chapter of this book examines the bust of the housing bubble in more detail. The collapse of the housing bubble was one of the major factors contributing to the economic crisis in the United States. In the years preceding the United States' housing bubble, monetary policy as employed by the Federal Reserve failed to impact long-term borrowing rates. A possible explanation for yield curve flattening and persistently low long-term interest rates is the fact that during this time period, the amount of United States debt being purchased by foreign holders increased. As long as foreign entities and individuals were willing to hold more U.S. debt, interest rates remained low. Low borrowing costs, and expanded use of non-conventional mortgages were associated with rapidly rising house prices, an issue which is explored in more detail. A case study on housing prices in the city of Los Angeles is presented as further evidence of the build-up and collapse of the housing bubble.

The fourth chapter of this volume examines contagion in financial crises by looking at stock market movements using a sample of 27 stock markets. Specifically, this chapter examines the issue of contagion while focusing on countries pre-crisis macroeconomic situations. There is evidence of contagion in two-thirds of the countries examined. Further, there is stronger evidence of contagion for countries with similar pre-crisis macroeconomic circumstances.

The final chapter of this text develops a theoretical model for examining contagion. Specifically, the model is capable of predicting contagion of both banking and currency crises. The theory presented highlights the dynamic aspects of contagion, indentifying when contagion is likely to be contemporaneous, when the spread of contagion is lagged, and when contagion of a crisis can be forward moving, resulting from an anticipated rather than realized crisis. From both the domestic and global perspective the current economic crisis is going to serve as a macroeconomic case study for decades to come. This text not only provides timely insight and analysis relevant for directing a robust recovery, but also serves as a historical record of this major global financial crisis.

In conclusion, we would like to express sincere gratitude to the contributors to this volume. This book would not be possible without their efforts, expertise, and exposition of these rapidly evolving and complex macroeconomic policy issues. Additionally, we would like to thank Nova Science Publishers Inc. for their efforts in the development of the book. Finally, we appreciate the financial support of the University of California at Los Angeles and Aoyama Gakuin University.

In: Financial Crisis in the Global … ISBN: 978-1-61740-597-0
Editors: A. Tomohara, M. Sherlock

Chapter 1

THE U.S. FINANCIAL CRISIS: ORIGINS, CONSEQUENCES, AND REMEDIES

Noha Emara and Marwa Hassan
Rutgers University, The State University of New Jersey, US
The Graduate Center, City University of New York, US

ABSTRACT

Policymakers and pundits have not shied away from using economic jargon while covering the United States' recent financial crisis. Language typically reserved for banking, finance, and economic policy experts has become commonplace. While the economic crisis has been widely covered, there is still much to be learned from this historical economic event. This chapter provides an overview of the recent financial crisis, focusing on explaining rather than simply presenting often intimidating crisis related economic jargon. The financial crisis has had destructive effects on the real economy. Specifically, expenditures on consumption and investment declined, total economic output fell, and unemployment rates reached double digits as the nation's economy fell victim to a prolonged recession. This study examines the origins and consequences of the 2007–2009 financial crisis as well as the subsequent policy responses undertaken in an effort to restore economic and financial stability. The study critically evaluates whether these policy measures were effective in gaining back consumer and investor confidence, ultimately preventing what has come to be known as the Great Recession from turning into another Great Depression.

I. INTRODUCTION

The financial crisis of 2007–2009 is not only the first major crisis of the 21st century, but also the most serious economic crisis since the Great Depression (1929 – 1933), as described by the National Bureau of Economic Research (NBER). According to the NBER, the U.S. economy officially entered into a recession in December 2007. However, economic conditions in the United States began deteriorating as early as August 2007. This chapter provides a comprehensive study of the current financial crisis.

The first portion of this chapter presents a clear overview of the origins of the crisis, highlighting issues such as the mismanagement of financial innovation, the housing bubble, and the subprime mortgage crisis. Some of the roots of the recent financial crisis can be traced back to policies employed in the wake to the 2001 recession, a recession that now appears to have been relatively mild.

Second, we examine the consequences of the recent financial crisis for the broader U.S. economy. One hallmark of this crisis was its breadth; the crisis had severely negative impacts on a variety of important economic sectors. The housing sector was badly affected by the high rate of defaults in subprime mortgages, associated with dramatic increases in home foreclosures and sharp housing price depreciations. Unable to distance itself from the housing sector meltdown, crisis in the financial sector resulted in a credit crunch. Unable to obtain access to credit, a number of large financial institutions faced huge losses and in some cases bankruptcy. The stock market reflected broader economic conditions; equity values declined dramatically while volatility increased significantly. Overall, the real economy crumbled as consumption and investment spending fell, along with total output. Unemployment increased dramatically as the United States became engulfed in the Great Recession.

The U.S. government responded to this crisis with a collection of aggressive and complementary policy actions. In this chapter, we review the different response measures implemented through fiscal and monetary policy measures. The chapter concludes by analyzing whether these policy measures effectively boosted consumer and investor confidence. The study concludes that there have been major improvements in many leading economic indicators. There has been a significant recovery in the stock market, a rise in investor confidence, an increase in the interest rate spread, an increase in money supply, and an increase in consumer spending on durable goods. Despite the relative improvement in consumer expectations regarding their own financial situation, consumers are not optimistic about improvements in labor market conditions. Consumers are also pessimistic about their ability to spend in the coming holiday season. This suggests that it might be too early to expect a lasting improvement in consumer confidence.

II. Origins of the Recent Financial Crisis

In order to construct a complete picture of the economy before it fell into the steep recession, this section introduces the confluence of factors that led up to the recent financial crisis. The roots can be traced back to policies employed in the wake to the 2001 recession, the subprime mortgage crisis, mismanagement of financial innovation, and the burst of the housing bubble.

1. The Fed's Remedy Package for the 2001 Recession and the Credit Boom

Shortly after the attacks of September 11, 2001, economists from the NBER announced that the economy had been in recession since March of that year. A confluence of factors contributed to this downturn: the dot-com bubble of the 1990s triggered a worldwide collapse in equity prices[1], federal monetary policy had been tightening, and the 2000 presidential elections sparked controversy and confusion. The Federal Reserve (Fed) had already responded to the onset of recession during the first half of 2001, easing credit to stimulate aggregate demand.

The Fed cut the federal funds rate from 6.5 percent to 3.5 percent over an eight-month period from January 2001 to August 2001. The federal funds rate is the market rate at which banks lend to each other overnight in order to meet their reserve requirements and other liquidity needs. The Fed sets a target for

[1] According to Kraay & Ventura (2007), between 1990 and the peak in mid 2000, equity prices increased nearly fivefold, and the growth rate of equity prices accelerated from 10.4 percent per year between 1990 and 1995 to 21.2 percent per year between 1995 and 2000, leading to rapid declines in investment and inventories, which accounted for the largest share of the decline in the U.S. economy.

this rate and buys and sells U.S. Treasury securities with the goal of achieving the target. The Fed announces the target rate to the public after every Federal Open Market Committee (FOMC) meeting, and the market reacts accordingly. The Fed's purchase of Treasury securities increases the money supply and reduces the federal funds rate, which encourages banks to extend more loans to the public. The fall in the cost of borrowing enhances consumption and investment, leading to higher levels of production and employment.

In order to avert a financial panic and liquidity shortage following the attacks of September 11, 2001, the Fed reduced the federal funds rate gradually until it reached one percent in June 2003. In addition, the Fed continued to reduce the discount rate, the rate at which it lends short-term funds to banks in order to provide liquidity to those banks suffering temporary reserve deficiency. Figures 1 to 3 show the behavior of the target and effective federal funds rate and the discount rate since 1982. It is clear that all rates reached their historically low levels throughout the period 2001 to mid 2004 as compared to their previous levels.

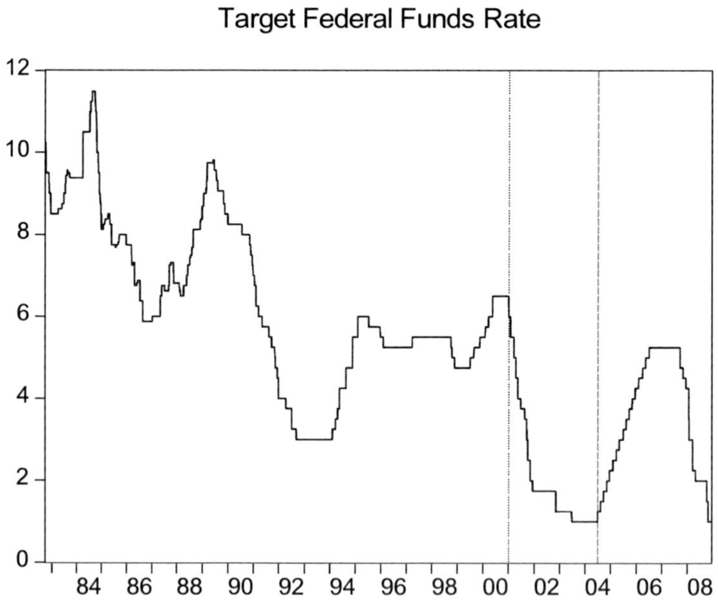

Source: Economic Research, Federal reserve bank of St. Louis http://sresearch.stlouisfed.org/fred2/

Figure 1. Target Federal Funds Rate, 1983-2009.

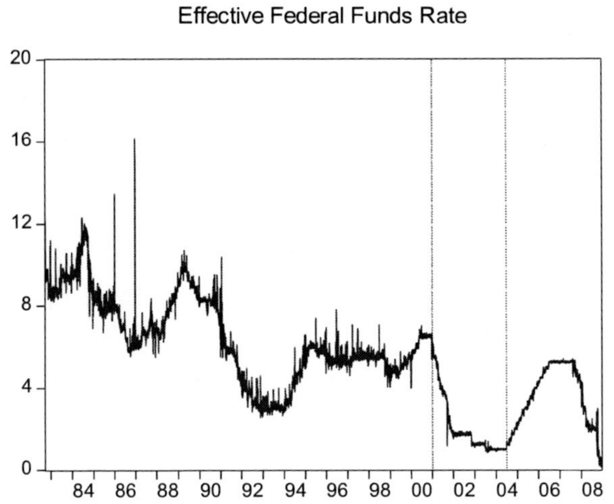

Source: Economic Research, Federal reserve bank of St. Louis http://research.stlouisfed.org/fred2/

Figure 2. Effective Federal Funds Rate, 1983-2009.

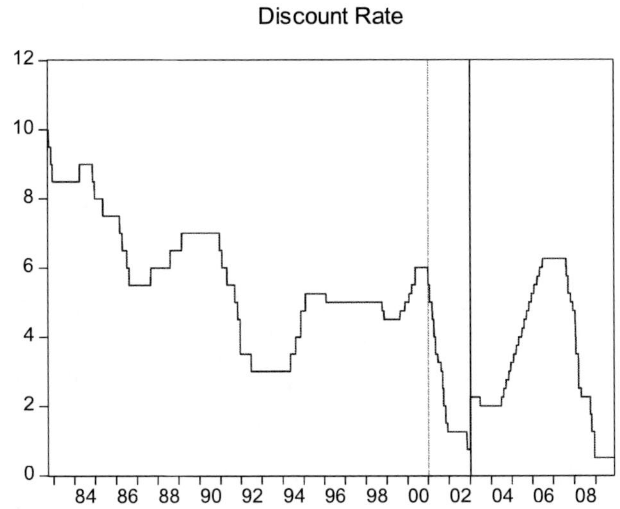

Source: Economic Research, Federal reserve bank of St. Louis http://research.stlouisfed.org/fred2/

Note: On January 9, 2003, The Fed discontinued the discount rate series and began to track the discount primary and secondary credit rates instead. The discount primary rate is shown in the graph after the dark line.

Figure 3. Discount Rate, 1983-2009.

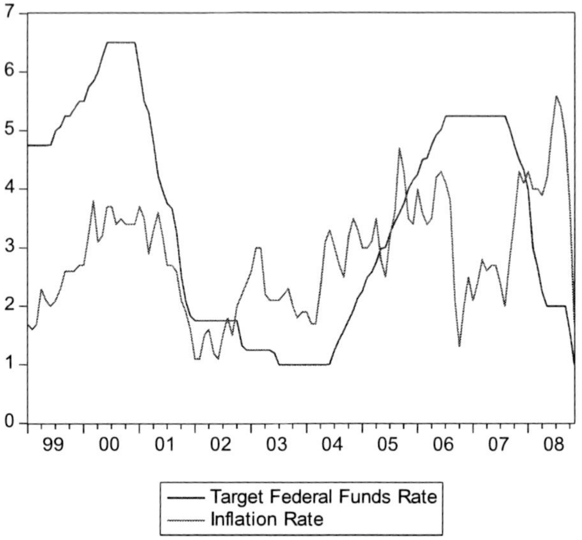

Sources: Economic Research, Federal reserve bank of St. Louis http://research.stlouisfed.org/fred2/, Bureau of Labor Statistics http://www.bls.gov/

Figure 4. Inflation rate and target federal funds rate, 1999-2008.

Sources: Economic Research, Federal reserve bank of St. Louis http://research.stlouisfed.org/fred2/, Bureau of Labor Statistics http://www.bls.gov/

Figure 5. Real interest rate, 1999-2008.

The historically low interest rates established by the Fed's expansionary monetary policy, which were also supported by massive official capital inflows from foreign investors, triggered a huge increase in U.S. private sector borrowing, the so-called credit boom, during the period from 2001 to 2005. A credit boom is defined as an episode in which credit to the private sector grows by more than its typical rate during a business cycle expansion. During the period from August 2002 to April 2005, the inflation rates were higher than the target federal funds rate, leading to negative real interest rates as reflected in Figure 4 and Figure 5.[2] In addition to the low cost of borrowing, favorable taxation treatments of certain debts induced U.S. households and financial institutions to bump up their financial leverage by borrowing more funds to finance their asset purchases.

The economy responded to these policy changes with a lag in time. The public response could not have been felt before the fourth quarter of 2001. The broadest measure of economic activity, the gross domestic product in constant dollars, rose four percent from its low in the third quarter of 2001, and it was 3.3% above its pre-recession peak in the fourth quarter of 2000. The economy began to expand steadily in 2002. Although timely action contained the short-run economic effects of the 2001 recession on the overall economy, these actions had an adverse impact in the long term.

2. Subprime Mortgages and Securitization

The majority of U.S. mortgage loans fall into the traditional prime category, representing eighty percent of all mortgage loans. These most prevalent loans are extended to borrowers with good credit who make traditional down payments and fully document their income. The remaining twenty percent of U.S. mortgages are considered nonprime and are offered to nonprime borrowers. These types of loans include the well-known subprime mortgages and Alt-A mortgages. Subprime lending represents a growing section of the mortgage market that expands the pool of credit to borrowers who are deemed the least credit worthy and would otherwise be denied credit. Borrowers who have a flawed credit history, cannot make the required down payment, or lack sufficient income in order to gain access to traditional lenders have flocked to subprime lenders. These borrowers are viewed as high risk;

---

[2] Real interest rates are interest rates adjusted for inflation. The real interest rate is calculated using the Fisher equation: Real interest rate = [(1+interest rate)/(1+inflation rate)] – 1.

they have to pay a higher interest rate than prime or better-qualified borrowers. Alternative – A (Alt-A) mortgages are near-prime mortgages, which are made to borrowers who appear to have good credit, but with limited or no income and asset verification. The subprime mortgages constituted fourteen percent of the U.S mortgage market as compared to only six percent for the Alt-A mortgages. This preponderance of subprime mortgages would explain why financial analysts would focus less on Alt-A mortgages.

The nonprime mortgages had grown rapidly from nine percent of newly originated securitized mortgages in 2001 to forty percent in 2006. The nonprime boom introduced an array of products that made it easier to obtain loans, such as:

balloon mortgages, in which the borrower only pays interest for the first ten or fifteen years, after which a large lump sum is due[3];

"no doc" or "low doc" loans, in which the lender accepts the borrower's stated income without any supporting documentation;

piggy-back loans, which eliminate the need for the typical twenty percent down payment by combining the first and second mortgages;

teaser loans or Adjusted Rate Mortgages (ARMs), in which the borrower may qualify for an artificially low interest rate for an initial term of, for example, two or three years, after which the rate adjusts—requiring higher payments that are less affordable for the borrower; and

stretch loans, in which the monthly payments represent more than fifty percent of the borrower's gross income [Nelson, 2003].

These new products opened the housing market to millions of Americans, pushing the home ownership rate from 63.8 percent in 1994 to a record 69.2 percent in 2004. The expansion of nonprime mortgages clearly played a role in the surge of homeownership. The growth of subprime lending in the past decade has been quite dramatic. The enormous growth in the share and size of subprime mortgage origination during the period from 2001 to 2007 is shown in Figure 6 and Figure 7. From 2004 to 2006, the subprime share of mortgage originations was around twenty percent; almost triple its share from 2001 to 2003. Total subprime loan originations have grown from $187 billion in 2001

[3] Balloon mortgages were not limited to nonprime borrowers; prime borrowers also had access to these types of mortgages. Borrowers would choose balloon mortgages if they planned on living in the house for a shorter period of time.

to $349 billion in 2003 to a peak of $663 billion in 2005 (The State of the Nation's Housing, 2008).

The financial markets have also increasingly securitized subprime loans. Securitization is the process by which most mortgage loans are sold to investors.[4] Thus, with the advent of securitization, banks issuing mortgages are no longer required to hold them to maturity and retain the default risk of borrowers. With the securitization process, banks follow the "originate to distribute" model, in which banks (the originators) essentially sell the mortgage loans to a third-party intermediary, which is either a Government-Sponsored Enterprise (GSE) such as Fannie Mae, Freddie Mac or Ginnie Mae, or a private-sector financial institution such as Countrywide Financial, Lehman Brothers, or Wells Fargo.[5]

The third-party intermediary often then packages the mortgage loans with other loans and sells the payment rights to investors. Some of the investors may use their payment rights to the mortgage loans to back other securities they issue. In this way, funds flow from investors through a third-party intermediary to banks and ultimately to individuals and families borrowing to buy houses. When the third-party intermediary sells bonds to investors and uses the funds to purchase mortgages from banks, banks are not only able to create more mortgages but also are relieved of the cost of monitoring borrowers.

[4] The American Securitization Forum (2003) defines securitization as the creation and issuance of debt securities, or bonds, whose payments of principal and interest derive from cash flows generated by separate pools of assets. In most cases, the originator of the asset anticipates a regular stream of payments. By pooling the assets together, the payment streams can be used to support interest and principal payments on debt securities. When assets are securitized, the originator receives the payment stream as a lump sum rather than spread out over time.

[5] GSEs are privately owned enterprises, but were chartered by Congress to expand the ability of residential mortgage finance by buying up mortgages from originators and holding and securitizing them. The implicit backing of the federal government enabled them to dominate the huge mortgage underwriting market and play a central role in the growth of mortgage securitization.

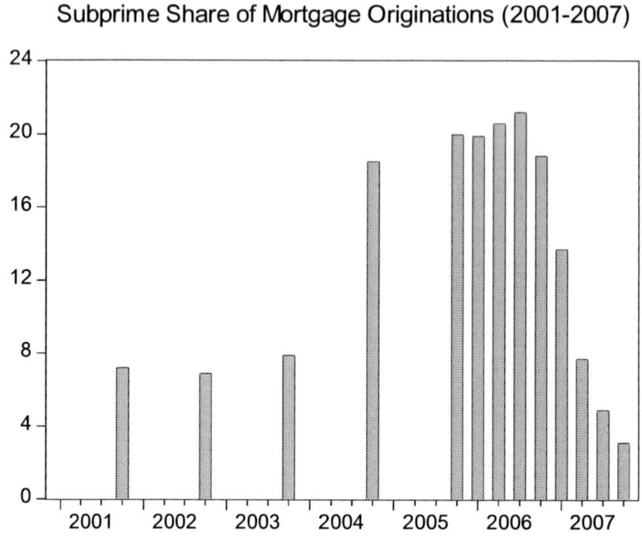

Source: The State of Nation's Housing, Joint Center for Housing Study, Harvard University. www.jchs.harvard.edu. Only end of year quarterly data are available for the years 2001-2005.

Figure 6. Subprime share percent of mortgage originations, 2001-2007.

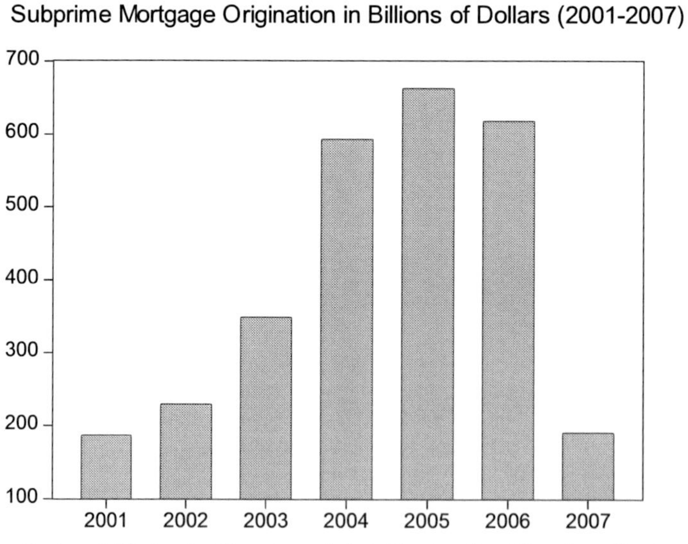

Source: The State of Nation's Housing, Joint Center for Housing Study, Harvard University. www.jchs.harvard.edu

Figure 7. Subprime mortgage originations in billions of dollars, 2001-2007.

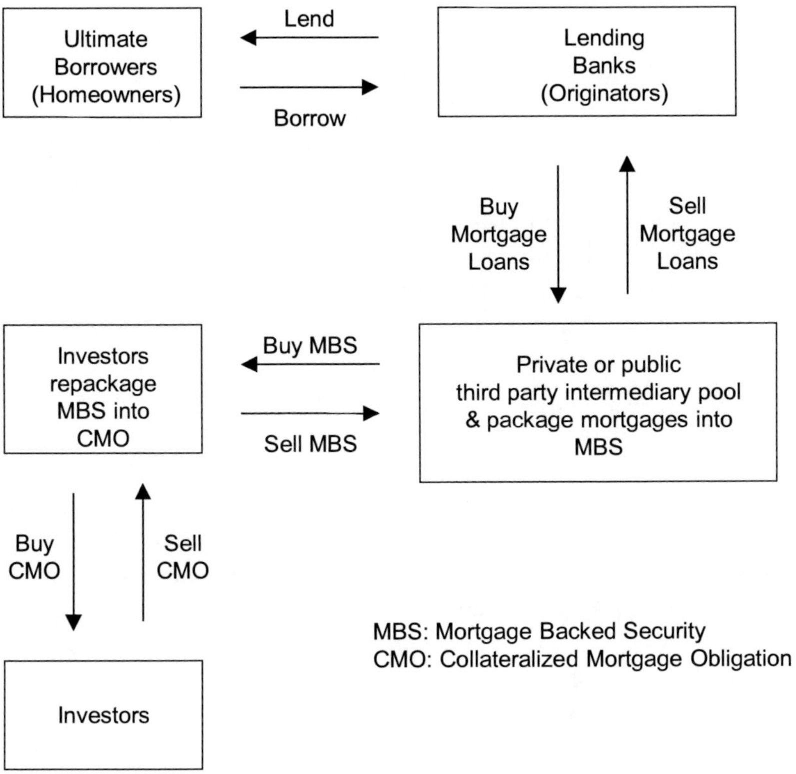

Figure 8. The securitization process.

Securitized mortgages are known as mortgage-backed securities (MBSs), while securitized assets—non-mortgage loans or assets with expected payment streams—are known as asset-backed securities (ABSs). As an example of an MBS issuance, assume that a bank has collected 100 mortgages, each worth \$150,000 with a 30-year maturity and a fixed interest rate of 5.50%. This \$15 million pool of mortgages can be used to back 100,000 bonds, each worth \$1,500 with a 30-year term and a fixed coupon rate of 5.00%. The MBSs are structured so that interest and principal payments from the mortgages in the pool are passed through to the owners of the security. Figure 8 illustrates the securitization process.

MBS investors suffer three major risks: interest rate risk, prepayment risk, and default risk. The interest rate risk leads to an opposite change in the value of the bonds as a result of a given change in interest rates. The prepayment risk arises when mortgages are prepaid without penalty. Prepayments introduce timing risk, since investors do not know when their bonds will be repaid, thereby eliminating future interest payments. Default risk is the risk that homeowners will default on the mortgages that back the MBS.

GSEs and private-sector MBS issuers use different tools to distribute default and payment timing risk, such as subordination, overcollateralization, and excess spread. Subordination refers to a securitization that issues multiple classes of bonds differing in bankruptcy priority. Some bonds are senior, while others are junior or subordinated. Senior bonds have a prior or superior claim on the issuer's assets and income than that of other subordinated bonds issued by the same entity. Therefore, senior bonds have priority in bankruptcy. When mortgages default, subordinated classes of bonds suffer the losses first.

Overcollateralization is the situation in which the asset pledged for a debt far exceeds the debt principle. Overcollateralization is measured as the difference between the principal balance on the loans in the pool and the principal balance on the outstanding MBSs. Excess spread is the difference between the interest payments coming in (loan payments minus servicing fees) and the weighted average payments going to bondholders. Excess spread can be used to build up overcollateralization. The first use of excess spread is to cover default losses. If any excess spread is left, it can be used to build up a cushion against future losses.

Collateralized mortgage obligation (CMO) is another form of MBS structured to allocate the timing of payments. A CMO includes an assortment of classes or tranches of bonds that offers a wide range of repayment dates. According to CMO, principal payments are allocated to the A bonds until completed. Then, principal payments would start being allocated to the B bonds.

3. Mismanagement of Financial Innovation

Financial innovation refers to the continuous development of financial products designed to achieve a particular client's objectives. Financial innovations range from introducing new mortgage loans, such as ARMs that mainly assist subprime borrowers in obtaining financing, to securitizing mortgages and other assets such as MBSs and ABSs in order to offset a particular risk exposure, such as a borrower's default.

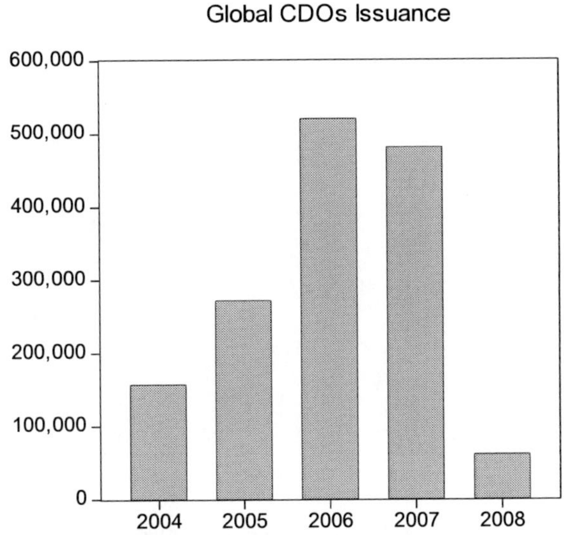

Source: SIFMA Securities Industry and Financial Markets Association http://www.sifma.org/research/pdf/CDO_Data2008-Q4.pdf

Figure 9. Global CDOs issuance.

Subprime lending growth is attributed to the spread of new products offering default protection, such as Collateralized Debt Obligation (CDO), which is a combination of MBSs in subprime mortgages and non-mortgage ABSs. Such CDOs divide the streams of income that flow from the underlying mortgages into tranches that absorb default losses according to a preset priority. This division appeals to different classes of investors with different tolerances for risk. Structured investment vehicles (SIVs) are similar to CDOs. The difference between SIVs and CDOs is essentially in the type of debt issued. The SIVs are structures backed by pools of assets, such as MBSs and CDO bonds. The SIVs issue short- and medium-term debt rather than the longer-term debt of most CDOs. The short-term debt is referred to as asset-backed commercial paper. Credit Default Swap (CDS) is another financial-instrument development that provides a hedge and protection from the risk of default for holders of MBSs, ABSs, and CDOs. Under CDSs, insurance companies and investment banks sell protection insurance to CDO investors that would pay out in the event of loan default.

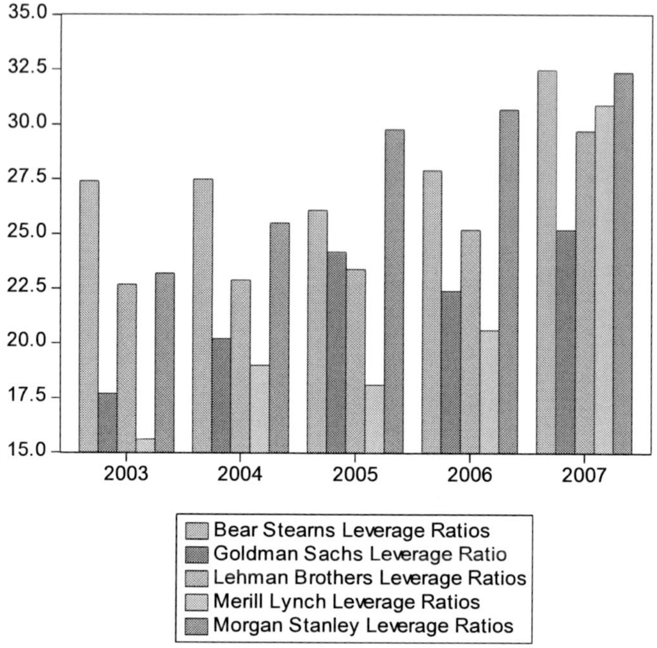

Source: Company annual reports.

Figure 10. Leverage Ratios of Major Investment Banks.

The spread of new bundles and combinations of MBSs and structured credit products required credit rating agencies such as Moody's and Standard and Poor's to rate these securities according to their risk profiles. By ordering the rights to the cash flows, the developers of CDOs (and subsequently other securities built on these structures) were able to convince the credit rating agencies to assign their highest ratings to the securities in the highest tranche or risk class. These ratings were believed to be justified because of risk-reducing factors. Such factors include credit default insurers and equity investors willing to bear the first losses. Figure 9 shows the global CDO issuance from 2004 to 2008, demonstrating an incredible increase in 2006.

The fact that credit rating agencies are paid by investment banks and other firms that organize and sell the structured securities to investors creates a conflict of interest. Thus, ratings agencies took part in fraud by bestowing their highest ratings on structured products created out of subprime loans. Banks around the world filled their vaults with these high-rated, structured products in order to benefit from the Basel II regulations on bank capital. Under the Basel II Accord, a bank holding triple-A (high rated) assets is allowed to keep less capital and is therefore able to make more loans. In addition, banks and investment firms were encouraged to purchase these securities because many of them were considered agency securities (issued by GSEs), implicitly backed by the government. Therefore, banks and investment firms have stocked up on these securities, especially CDOs.

These new financial instruments prospered in the low interest rate settings supported by the Fed's easy monetary policy and poor regulatory oversight. Thus, financial institutions borrowed more and more money to finance their purchases of mortgage-related securities. This borrowing led large investment banks to greatly increase their leverage ratios. Figure 10 shows the change in leverage ratios of the largest five investment banks in the U.S. during the period from 2003 to 2007.

4. Housing Boom and Bust

Homeownership has always been a way to achieve the American dream. Moreover, by owning their homes, financially capable U.S. households can save on taxes and earn a solid investment return. As a consequence of the dot-com crash and the subsequent credit boom, with borrowing at historically low levels of interest rates, household investment in real estate became more attractive. Real estate became a safe alternative to the stock market, especially for investors and speculators who were hit hard in the dot-com crash. Government intervention also played an important role in increasing the demand for home ownership. In 2002, the Department of Housing and Urban Development imposed "affordable housing quotas" on Fannie Mae and Freddie Mac in order to increase their holdings of subprime mortgages.

By 2003, these conditions helped to create a stretched housing market. A dramatic increase in housing prices ensued as buyers with access to low-cost mortgage credit competed in bidding wars. With little or no money down required, great incentives to enter the housing market existed. It appeared that buying a house would definitely yield a return, since housing prices had been increasing continuously during the housing bubble. The relaxation of traditional requirements for borrowing a mortgage opened an easy profit opportunity to almost everyone. Buying a house was no longer considered a long-term investment; many people during the housing boom believed they could "flip" their house value within a year or two and literally make capital gains. Some of these borrowers were able to "invest" by borrowing from lenders who were willing to take on more risk of default with a higher return on the subprime mortgages.

The relaxation of underwriting requirements and the advent of mortgage products that initially reduced borrowers' payments, together with the unprecedented availability of mortgage credit to speculators, investors, and homebuyers with past credit problems, helped to fuel the boom. By channeling the funds of institutional investors to support the origination of subprime mortgages, many households previously unable to qualify for mortgage credit became eligible for loans. This new group of eligible borrowers increased housing demand and helped inflate home prices. From the fourth quarter of 2002 to the fourth quarter of 2006, real house prices rose by an additional 31.6 percent, an annual rate of 7.1 percent. For the first time, median home prices across the nation increased many times more quickly than monthly incomes for several years in a row. Figure 11 shows this.

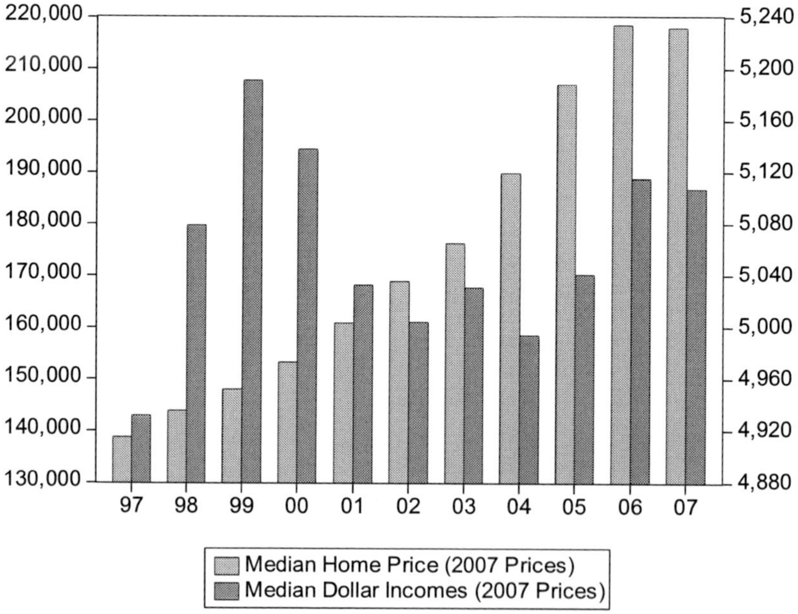

Source: The State of Nation's Housing, Joint Center for Housing Study, Harvard University. www.jchs.harvard.edu

Figure 11. Trends in U.S. inflation-Adjusted Median Home Prices and Median Monthly Incomes in U.S. dollars, 1997-2007.

The run-up in housing prices created a bubble that soon had to burst for two main reasons: excessive supply in the housing market and subprime turmoil. The bizarre increase in housing prices made homeowners feel increasingly wealthy. This "wealth effect" created a boom of all sorts of private consumption, and spending increased beyond incomes, specifically when homeowners used the equity in their homes through home equity loans to get more cash to spend. The overall increase in demand led to an overall increase in price levels in terms of rising inflation. Thus, the Fed started to raise the interest rates in June 2004, fearing the price that might have to be paid through inflation. This change in the Fed's policy can be seen in Figure 4 above. By 2005, higher borrowing costs and skyrocketing home prices were slowing homebuyer demand in some markets, and the demand for new houses faded. Meanwhile builders continued to build new houses to meet the (no longer) increased demand. More and more vacant new houses were listed on the market.

In the meantime, investments in subprime loans were considered safe ventures because housing prices were appreciating so quickly. Consequently, investors eager for higher returns borrowed short-term money from banks in order to purchase securities backed by subprime mortgages. At the same time, the spread of new financial instruments that slice and bundle cash flows associated with MBSs and ABSs in the form of CDOs obscured the impact of deterioration in loan performance on bond issues. In anticipation of further profits, financial investors leveraged their investments and exposed themselves to refinancing risk each time they had to roll over their debt.

Lenders and investors continued to accumulate tiers of risk without taking into account the likely cost of their reckless actions if the future outcome were to deviate from their expectations. Rising interest rates led to higher borrowing costs. The increase in mortgage rates coincided with the reset dates of many adjustable-rate subprime loans. At that point, borrowers with these loans started to witness increases in monthly mortgage payments. Subprime homeowners were the most vulnerable segment of the population. They had no access to deep pockets or sufficient equity against which to borrow in order to meet these higher payments. As a result, many subprime homeowners had little choice but to default on their mortgages. Defaults on subprime loans increased. With mounting excess in the supply of housing and the temporary boost from mortgage product innovations coming to an end, nominal housing prices started to drop in the third quarter of 2006. This drop eradicated the shield offered by high rates of home price appreciations and enlarged the segment of distressed borrowers.

The spread of defaults in the subprime market led to a severe reduction in the valuation of MBSs and CDOs, which contained substantial quantities of subprime mortgages and had a devastating impact on credit availability and liquidity. No longer buying new originations, mortgage investors quickly exited the markets and tried to sell their positions in existing loans in a market with little demand. Losing confidence in some investment funds and mortgage companies, investors demanded repayment of their short-term borrowings using insuring instruments, such as the CDSs. This cycle imposed huge losses on financial institutions and insurance companies. Lenders responded by tightening credit in the second half of 2007, depressing the market with the risk of an extended housing downturn. This squeeze led to the so-called "credit crunch."

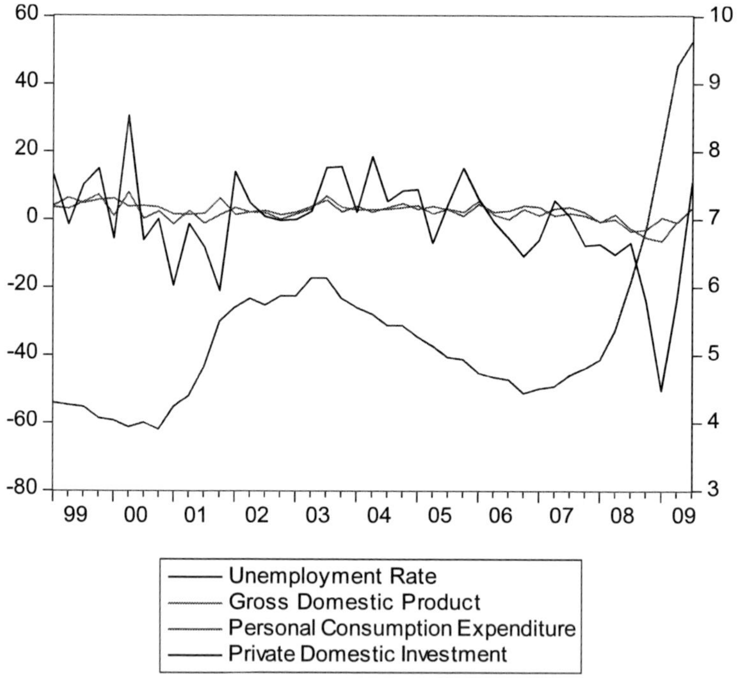

Source: Bureau of Economic Analysis, http://www.bea.gov/national/nipaweb

Notes: The left scale depicts the Gross Domestic Product, Personal Consumption Expenditure and Private Domestic Investment while the right scale depicts the unemployment rate.

Figure 12. Percentage Change From Preceding Period in Economic Variables.

III. Consequences of the Recent Financial Crisis

This Section tracks the outcomes that ensued from the aforementioned causes of the crisis. The combination of all outcomes led to destructive effects in the real economy in terms of declining expenditure on consumption, investment, total output, and high rates of unemployment, thus engulfing the economy in a recession as represented in Figure 12.

The 2007-2008 "credit crunch," defined by a severe shortage of money and credit, was initially caused by a loss of confidence by investors in the U.S. mortgage and credit markets. It resulted in a global liquidity crisis due to the close interaction of banking institutions around the world. Causing severe repercussions in the U.S. economy since its advent in August 2007, the crunch led to a serious economic slowdown through its impact on the housing market, the banking sector, and the stock market.

1. The Housing Market

The increasingly excessive supply of housing along with declining home prices increased the flood of foreclosures, since banks are generally anxious to sell properties on which they have foreclosed. The supply of housing inventory today remains very high relative to sales, and given the rapidly deteriorating economy, housing prices have continued to decline in 2009.

Because of the rising tension in financial markets, the demand for housing has diminished, since banks are far more reluctant to make loans now than they were in the prior two years. Banks resort to far more stringent checks and standards before approving loans. Plenty of potential borrowers who had been eligible to receive loans in 2006 became unable to qualify for a loan under the new rigid standards. As a result, the number of potential buyers has tapered substantially over the last two years, leading to further declines in housing prices in many markets. In the first quarter of 2008, housing prices were falling at an average national rate of twenty percent and at more than thirty percent annually in the most rapidly deflating markets such as Las Vegas, Los Angeles, and Phoenix. In December 2008, national housing prices fell 11.1 percent from the year before. By the end of 2008, the total value of residential properties was $19.1 trillion, down $2.4 trillion from $21.5 trillion in December of 2007 [Mackenzie 2009].

This loss of homeowners' housing wealth continues to put significant stress on consumers' balance sheets, particularly as job losses continue to grow. In addition, the sharp decline in consumer spending on houses, autos, and other durables, following the acute drop in lending to households, caused a recession in the construction sector. This was felt especially in new houses, as well as declines in the production of consumer durables. Consumer spending on appliances has also dropped. All these consequences pushed the U.S. economy deeper into recession. Unemployment rates reached 10.2 percent as of October 2009, the highest in 26 years according to the Bureau of Labor Statistics. Figure 12 shows the rising trend of unemployment rates since the advent of the credit crunch and the declining pattern in the growth rate of private consumption and GDP.

2. The Banking Sector

The accelerated decline in U.S. housing prices, along with the rising defaults in subprime mortgages, reduced the values of both MBSs and CDOs. This forced banks and financial institutions holding these securities to write-down their assets and bad loans, thus deteriorating their balance sheets.[6] Writing-down bad loans is considered a critical cut in bank capital, thus deepening the recession and increasing unemployment. The ongoing fall in bank capital due to writing down bad loans pushed banks to deleverage by selling their assets and to cut back sharply on their lending to households and businesses. This is because they must keep their lending in proportion to the new lower levels of their capital base.

Banks around the world have already written off losses of more than $200 billion in connection with the collapse of the housing market. The April 2009 issue of the Global Financial Stability Report (GFSR) estimates that, subject to a number of assumptions, credit write-downs on U.S.-originated assets by all holders since the start of the crisis total $2.7 trillion. In the next two years, total write-downs could reach $4 trillion, approximately two-thirds of which may be taken by banks. Those capital losses caused financial institutions to become insolvent and pushed them to either file bankruptcy or undergo forced mergers with stronger banks.

To illustrate, we provide a summary of the important global and domestic financial failures since the onset of the crisis. In February 2007, Freddie Mac announced that it will no longer buy the most risky subprime mortgages and

[6] A write-down occurs when banks and financial institutions reduce the book value of an asset, if is overstated compared to current market values.

mortgage-related securities. In June 2007, Moody's and Standard and Poor's downgraded over 100 bonds backed by second-lien subprime mortgages. This action led to a freeze in the asset-backed commercial paper market. In August 2007, BNP Paribas, France's largest investment bank, suspended redemption of shares held in some of its money market funds. In the same month, Fitch Ratings downgraded Countrywide Financial Corporation to its lowest investment-grade ratings. All this led the European Central Bank and the Fed to inject huge funds to ensure the liquidity of the financial system. However, banks responded by increasing their reserves rather than lending to each other. The shortage of credit led to the failure, in September 2007, of the fifth largest mortgage lender in the United Kingdom, Northern Rock, which had relied on wholesale short-term borrowing rather than deposits for its funding.

The ramifications of the credit crunch were observed in the U.S. during 2008. In March 2008, Bear Stearns, the fifth largest bank, which invested heavily in the subprime-related securities, was acquired by JP Morgan Chase for less than five percent of what it was worth one year earlier. In July 2008, the Fed and the Treasury had to purchase GSE obligations and reformed the regulatory supervisions of Fannie Mae and Freddie Mac. These GSEs had insured over $5 trillion of mortgages or MBSs assets and were suffering sizable losses from their holdings of subprime securities.

September 2008 marked the black month of the year, in which most of the huge failures occurred. Merill Lynch and Lehman Brothers, the third and the fourth largest investment banks in the U.S., respectively, suffered substantial losses in the subprime market. While Merill Lynch publicized its sale to Bank of America for a price less than 60% of its value a year earlier, Lehman Brothers filed for bankruptcy. Consequently, the net asset value of shares in the Reserve Primary Money Fund, a large money market mutual fund, fell below $1. This fall was caused primarily by losses on Lehman Brothers commercial papers and medium-term notes. The federal government seized Washington Mutual (WAMU), the sixth largest bank in the U.S., and sold it to JPMorgan Chase. Wells Fargo purchased Wachovia Corporation without requiring assistance from the federal government.

In the meantime, insurance companies also suffered liquidity problems. The American International Group (AIG) suffered an acute liquidity tragedy following a downgrade in its credit rating. AIG had been one of the largest players in the market for credit default swaps in which AIG had to make payouts on possible losses from subprime mortgage securities. AIG had almost $600 billion of gross national exposure in "super senior" credit derivatives, including $80 billion tied to subprime mortgages. The Fed extended a total of $173 billion in loans to AIG to keep the company afloat.

The cutback of lending also threatened very short-term loans, which banks and other institutions make to each other in order to produce working capital. Corporations, finance companies, and banks rely on investors for the cash they deposit into money market funds and other short-term investment vehicles. Ultimately, this cash buys the commercial paper issued to help fund everything from corporate payrolls to a manufacturing company's production inventories. If the short-term commercial paper and money markets were to break down, the economy could go into a severe collapse; solvent and profitable businesses would be unable to attract working capital. Higher levels of unemployment would occur as well. In addition, major investment projects, such as acquisition of new buildings and major machinery, are being scaled back. Some major nonfinancial companies were affected and went bankrupt as well. Figure 12 also shows the decline in investments during the credit crunch period.

3. The Stock Market

Stock markets are a central link between the financial world and the real economy. Stock prices are fundamental to the functioning of a market-based economy. They signify the value of the companies that issued the stock and how those companies allocate scarce resources. For individuals, stocks are one way we choose to hold our wealth. When stock values rise, stockholders get richer; when they fall, stockholders get poorer. These changes affect consumption and saving patterns, generating fluctuations in economic activity. Stock market indexes are designed to show how much the value of an average stock has changed and how much total wealth has increased or decreased.

High stock prices would simply indicate that investors are bidding up the prices, because they have confidence in the market and are expecting the companies to be profitable. Figure 13 below shows the behavior of the major U.S. stock indexes—S&P 500, Dow Jones Industrial Average, and Nasdaq Composite—throughout the last decade. The figure indicates how the three indexes dropped sharply and entered into a bear market in the summer of 2008, marking their lowest levels in May 2009.

The stock market has fallen by about forty percent since October 2007. This decline is estimated to have wiped out $2.5 trillion from households' net worth [Mackenzie 2009]. Declines in household wealth reduces consumption, because households need to save more to make up for lost wealth and thereby maintain their standard of living in future years. The collapse of the stock market also leads to sharp declines in real investment, distorting the economic decisions that companies make and making it more difficult to raise financing for new projects.

The outcome of the previous discussion leads us to highlight the channels through which the financial crisis affects the real economy, in the form of declining levels of production and employment. There are five different transmission channels of the financial crisis: the wealth effect, the confidence effect, the credit channel effect, the multiplier effect, and the effect of state and local governments.

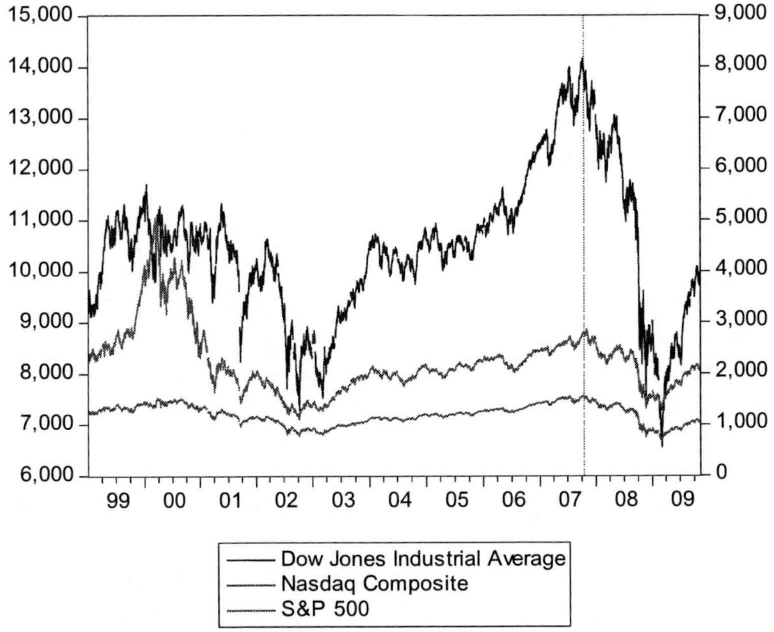

Source: New York Stock Exchange.

Notes: The left scale depicts the Dow Jones Industrial Average Index, while the right scale depicts the Nasdaq Composite and the S&P 500.

Figure 13. Performance of Major U.S. Stock Indexes (1999–2009).

The wealth effect, evidenced in declining household wealth due to the loss in housing values and the massive declines in stock prices, has a direct impact on consumption. Consumption falls as households resort to more savings to offset their lost wealth and to maintain their living standards in the future.

The confidence effect can be seen as the lost confidence of the ordinary consumer and investor, reflected in their declining consumption and investment spending. The confidence effect is directly related to the wealth effect: the larger the amount of lost wealth, the less confidence consumers and investors will have in their financial transactions. Their increased caution ultimately has a negative impact on spending.

The credit channel effect, outlined in the credit crunch section above, results in liquidity shortage and tightening credit standards, further depressing and adversely affecting business activity and consumption. The typical multiplier effect magnifies the impact of the wealth, confidence, and credit channel effects. When firms and households reduce their spending because of any of these channels, demand for consumption and investment goods decreases, firms reduce their payrolls and investments, and employees and suppliers respond by reducing their spending, and so on.

The effect on state and local governments is usually witnessed when states announce cuts to their social expenditure on welfare programs, education, and health care in order to balance their budgets when they experience difficulties with borrowing.

Though state and local governments may participate in spreading the strain of the financial crisis, the federal government has initiated policy actions in an attempt to restore overall economic and financial stability. The next section discusses the different complementary policy measures taken by the government and the Fed in order to boost aggregate spending, ease the strain in the credit market, and pull the economy out of recession.

IV. Remedies to the Recent Financial Crisis

This section introduces and discusses how the U.S. government responded to the recent financial crisis with a collection of aggressive and complementary policy actions. In this section, we review the different response measures implemented through fiscal and monetary policy measures. This section concludes with a critical evaluation of whether these policy measures were effective in gaining back consumer and investor confidence, ultimately preventing what has come to be known as the Great Recession from turning into another Great Depression.

1. Policy Responses to Restore Economic and Financial Stability

By the middle of 2008, the U.S. economy showed many signs of heading into a recession. Significant declines in production, employment, real income, building permits, vendor performance, and other indicators occurred for several months. In December 2008, the NBER announced that "the nation's economy peaked, and the recession began, in December 2007."

The recession required very comprehensive, forceful, and emphatic measures in order to prevent the U.S. economy from going into another depression. Many measures were taken through fiscal and monetary policies, which complemented each other to form one package to pull the economy out of recession. Measures taken include the following: many cuts in the discount rate from early 2007 until now, reductions in the target federal funds rate starting in mid-2007, extensions of various lending programs to companies and institutions in need starting in 2008, expansions in the Fed balance sheet starting in mid-2008, provisions of liquidity to the private sector in late 2008, and both of the fiscal stimulus plans passed in early 2008 and early 2009.

The Fed's objective during this period has been to reduce the cost of borrowing in order to encourage private consumption and investment spending, leading to higher levels of production and employment. To achieve this goal, the Fed bought government bonds to reduce the federal funds rate, increasing the money supply and affecting short-term interest rates in the desired direction. The Fed took action by reducing the targeted federal funds rate in steps from 5.25 percent in August 2007 to around zero percent by December 2008. In addition, the Fed supported this action by imposing further reductions in the discount rate, from 5.75 percent in August 2007 to 0.5 percent in October 2009.

In December 2007, when conventional monetary policy tools were deemed insufficient to control the squeezed liquidity in the market, the Fed announced the use of an unconventional measure called the Term Auction Facility (TAF). Through TAF, term funds were auctioned to depository institutions as a way to create more short-term funding in the interbank market. The Fed also announced that it would buy up to $100 billion in debts issued by housing related GSEs and up to $500 billion in agency-guaranteed backed securities. These measures, however, were not enough to increase liquidity in the financial market, especially after the collapse of Bear Stearns Asset Management in July 2008. In response, the Fed made the unprecedented decision to reduce the targeted federal funds rate twice during the month of January, from one percent to 0.75 percent, then to 0.5 percent.

To stabilize the breakdown of the commercial paper market, in September 2008 the Treasury announced a temporary insurance program, and the Fed announced the creation of a backstop commercial paper. The Fed bought three-month unsecured and asset-backed commercial paper directly from struggling financial institutions. Moreover, the Fed expanded old temporary swap lines and established new ones with twelve foreign central banks in order to stabilize the global financial market, which in turn affects the U.S. financial market.

In a measure to stabilize housing prices, the U.S. government took over the two mortgage giants Freddie Mac and Fannie Mae on September 7, 2008. These two companies held about $5 trillion in obligations, a significant amount that they could not handle, given the 18 percent drop in housing prices from 2006. The U.S. treasury invested $100 billion in each company to back their assets.

In November 2008, further action was taken to stabilize the financial system by announcing the Temporary Liquidity Guarantee Program (TLGP). The main objectives of this program are to increase confidence in the market and to stabilize the financial system by guaranteeing newly issued unsecured debts. These debts are unsecured in the sense that the lender provides money to the borrower without the security that the loan is backed by any underlying asset. The lender is then discouraged from providing their funds to the borrower, especially under the current state of the economy.

Another important objective of the TLGP is to provide full coverage of non-interest-bearing deposits above $250,000, regardless of dollar amount, until December 31, 2009. Under this provision, the depository institution pays no interest on the deposit and in turn does not reserve any right requiring advance notice before withdrawals.

Owing to the severity of the recession, fiscal policy actions were adopted to complement the monetary policy actions. In February 2008, President Bush signed the Economic Stimulus Act that contained many tax cuts and rebates for households and businesses. The bill offered a tax rebate of $600 per person, which increased aggregate demand. Furthermore, in response to the subprime mortgage crisis and with the purpose of increasing liquidity in the secondary mortgage market, the government passed the Emergency Economic Stabilization Act of 2008, the so-called "bailout plan." The main goal of this act was to strengthen investors' confidence in the market by authorizing the government to buy $700 billion of illiquid MBSs.

In addition, the Housing and Economic Recovery Act was passed in July 2008 to help borrowers at risk of losing their homes by providing affordable government-insured mortgages. The main objective of this act was to address the subprime mortgage crisis and restore confidence in the housing market.

To further ease the stress on the market after the failure of Lehman Brothers, President Bush signed the Troubled Asset Relief Program (TARP) in October 2008 —part of the Emergency Economic Stabilization Act of 2008— with a maximum authorization of $700 billion for buying many of the MBSs and other troubled assets. In addition, in January 2009 the central bank pledged to buy $500 billion of the MBSs backed by Fannie Mae, Freddie Mac, and Ginnie Mae.

Additional fiscal actions were taken in February 2009 when President Obama signed the American Recovery and Reinvestment Act (ARRA), which included a variety of government spending programs focusing spending primarily on education, health care, and infrastructure. The act also included tax cuts and the expansion of unemployment benefits and other social welfare provisions.

In sum, there have been many sets of tools used by the Fed to prevent the economy from going into a depression. Besides reducing the federal funds rate, which reached almost zero percent in December 2008, the Fed has applied other monetary tools ranging from conventional to unconventional practices. The first set of tools related to the provision of short-term liquidity for large financial institutions. The second set of tools included the direct provision of liquidity to borrowers and investors. Finally, the third set of tools related to the purchase of longer-term securities for the Fed's portfolio. It is evident that the second and third sets of tools are essentially unconventional, but they are nonetheless important and required for the support of the functionality of the credit market. In addition to monetary policy tools, fiscal policies were also needed to complement monetary actions. The consensus among economists is that fiscal policy should focus more on long-term goals and leave short-term goals to be covered by monetary policy. However, the severe recession has created the need for a fiscal stimulus that works hand-in-hand with monetary tools in order to increase aggregate spending and thereby boost output and employment. The deficit of the fiscal year ending on September 30, 2009, hit a record $1.4 trillion and, according to Paul Krugman (2009), "This spending was what avoided a repetition of the Great Depression."

Having discussed the policy responses to the recent U.S. financial crisis, the next section analyzes the effectiveness of these responses in restoring economic and financial stability and in gaining back consumers' and investors' confidence in the market.

2. Policy Measures Analysis

By August 2009, the U.S. economy showed some signs that it was recovering from the recession. The GDP started to grow after four consecutive quarters of decline, U.S. mortgage rates started to decline in Fall 2009, activities in securitization markets picked up, short-term funding markets were functioning more smoothly, corporate bond issuance remained strong, consumer durable spending started to pick up from it s significant negative growth, and most of the leading economic indicators show signs of hope. More specifically, major U.S. stock indexes started to show positive growth, money supply increased significantly, the interest rate spread started to increase, and consumer confidence strengthened to some degree. These indicators suggest that the recession had reached bottom and that there was a good possibility of growth.

As discussed in the previous section, the policies of the Fed and the government in response to the 2007–2009 U.S. financial crisis have been quite aggressive, complementary, and comprehensive. There is no doubt that the situation would have been much worse if there had been no such responses. Besides the conventional monetary policy tools, the Fed implemented many unconventional tools to ease the liquidity in the credit market. To complement these actions through fiscal policy, the government implemented many tax cuts and rebates in addition to increasing its spending to simulate the aggregate demand. However, there have been many doubts about the effectiveness of the fiscal policy in dealing with the recent crisis in a timely manner. An econometric study by Christina Romer, the chair of the Council of Economic Advisers, and Jared Bernstein (2009), an advisor to Vice President Biden, estimates that a one percent increase in government expenditure would lead to an increase in output by 1.5 percent in two years. On the other hand, their study shows that a one percent tax cut would lead to a one percent increase in GDP in two years. The Romer and Bernstein model was challenged by Cogan et al. (2009), who used an alternative New Keynesian model to prove that a one percent increase in government expenditure would lead to a GDP increase of only 0.5 percent after two years. This model implies that the well known multiplier effect is very low during periods of recession due to the loss of consumer and investor confidence.

The impacts of these responses on the U.S. economy are analyzed in this section by looking at the key economic indicators. Most economists use the Leading Economic Indicator (LEI) index in analyzing and forecasting short-run economic fluctuations. This index attempts to forecast when the economy will go in and out of a period of growth or recession. The consensus is that the LEI will provide an indication six to nine months prior to a change in the economy. The LEI index consists of ten data series and is measured by the Conference Board. The data series include the average workweek of production workers in manufacturing, the average initial weekly claims for unemployment insurance, new orders for consumer goods and materials adjusted for inflation, new orders for nondefense capital goods, the index of supplier deliveries, new building permits issued, the index of stock prices, the money supply adjusted for inflation, the interest rate spread, and the index of consumer expectations.

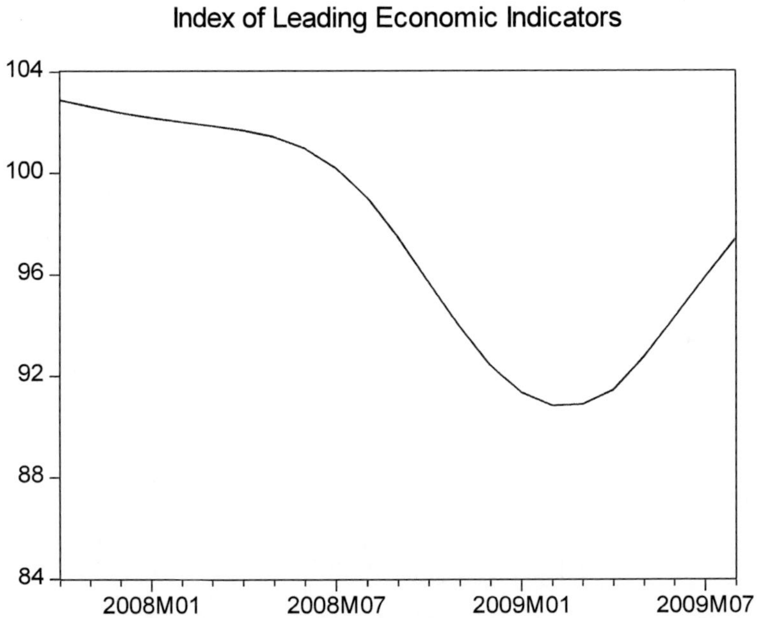

Source: Organization for Economic Co-operation and Development (OECD), http://stats.oecd.org/Index.aspx?DataSetCode=MEI_CLI

Figure 14. Index of leading economic indicators.

By analyzing the index of LEI from October 2007 to August 2009, Figure 14 below shows a drop starting from the onset of the crisis until it reached its lowest point in February 2009; the index then started to rise over the subsequent six consecutive months until it reached about 97 points in August 2009. This rise represents an increase of about 73 percent.

Based on historical behavior, the LEI index should turn downward a few months to a year before each recession, and it should also turn upward just before the end of a recession, as it did during almost every U.S. recession from 1970 through 2001. The 73 percent increase in the LEI index from February to August 2009 is considered a sign of the end of the recession.

To analyze the effectiveness of recent monetary and fiscal policy measures in regaining consumer and investor confidence in the market, this section provides a brief analysis of the behavior of stock prices, consumer expectations, money supply, and interest rate spread during the 2007–2009 period.

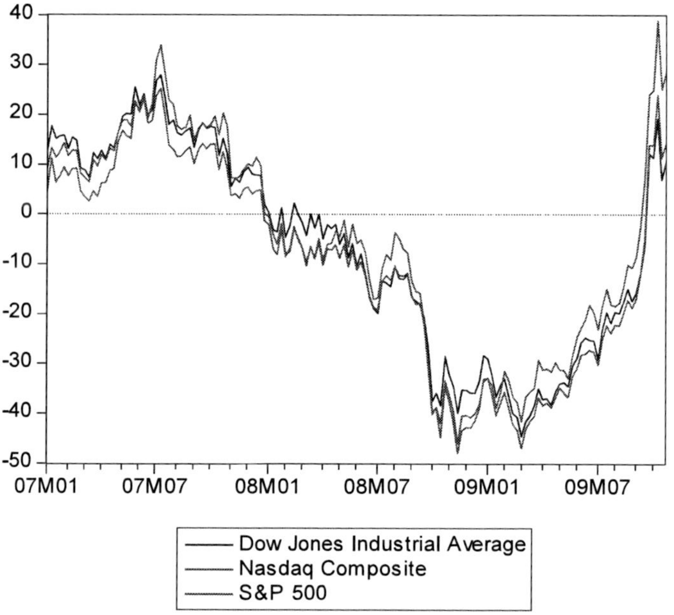

Source: New York Stock Exchange.

Figure 15. Major U.S. Stock Indexes, Percentage change from 52 weeks earlier.

First, the variability in stock prices is an indication of what investors expect in terms of future market conditions. As mentioned in the previous section, high stock prices would simply indicate that investors, because of their confidence in the market and their expectation that companies will be profitable, are bidding up prices. Figure 15 shows the percentage change of the major U.S. stock indexes: S&P, Dow Jones, and Nasdaq. Generally moving together, the three indexes dropped sharply and entered into a bear market in the summer of 2008. The indexes marked their lowest negative growth levels in the period from November 2008 through May 2009. Many factors contributed to the negative growth experienced by the three major U.S. stock indexes. The most important factors were the bankruptcy declared by the investment bank Lehman Brothers, the forced merger of Merrill Lynch with Bank of America, and the concerns about the ability of AIG to stay capitalized.

In the period thereafter, the three indexes revealed a positive average growth rate of about seventeen percent by the end of October 2009. This rate signaled a rise in investor confidence in the market. The continuous reduction in the federal funds rate, to the extent that it reached a target level of zero to 25 basis points in 2009, had contributed to this recovery. The drop in the federal funds rate has direct and indirect effects on the stock market. The most obvious direct effect is the drop in the cost for banks to borrow from the Fed. The indirect effects, on the other hand, are reflected by the impact on individuals and businesses. For individuals, a drop in the federal funds rate will lead to a drop in the cost for individuals to borrow from the banks. More specifically, interest rates for individuals' credit cards and mortgages will drop. This drop in turn increases individual spending and leads to an increase in business profits. As profits increase, stock prices increase as well. However, the drop in the federal funds rate did not contribute to increasing consumer borrowing. With rising unemployment and continued tightening of credit conditions, consumer borrowing fell by $14.8 billion in September 2009.

Businesses are more directly affected by the drop in the federal funds rate. As their cost of borrowing from the banks decreases, they are able to grow and increase their profits. Also, a decrease in the federal funds rate has a positive indirect effect on a company's stock price.[7] As a company's debt expenses fall because of the lowered federal funds rate, company spending increases on project expansions, which produce higher profits. This cycle will finally lead to an increase in the stock price. Accordingly, the drop in the federal funds rate has largely contributed to the increase in the stock prices that we have seen since the first quarter of 2009.

With regard to the second component of the LEI index to be analyzed, consumers' expectations, there was major deterioration in consumer confidence in the market, which worsened as the crisis unfolded. Many factors have contributed to this loss of consumer confidence: the increased volatility

---

[7] The stock price is equal to the sum of the future discounted cash flows divided by the number of shares available. The price of a stock fluctuates based on people's expectations of the company at different times.

in financial markets; the drop in housing prices, which affected consumers' wealth; the deteriorating macroeconomic conditions; the failure of large financial firms; and the major securities scandals. Accordingly, there arose a real need for polices to strengthen consumer confidence in the market.

Consumer confidence is measured by the consumer sentiment index, calculated on a monthly basis by the University of Michigan. The index consists of 50 questions administered through telephone interviews in all U.S. states excluding Hawaii and Alaska. The questions are designed to focus on how consumers regard their own financial situation, according to the short- and long-term conditions of the economy. An increase in this index implies an increase in consumer confidence in the market, which is reflected in an increase in their demand for goods and services and results in an increase in output.

Figure 16 shows the behavior of the consumer sentiment index. The figure indicates that this index started to decline from early 2007 to late 2008. Not until the beginning of 2009, as the stock market substantially recovered and as the credit spread narrowed, did the consumer sentiment index begin to pick up, with an average growth of about 2.4 percent over the months of 2009 as compared to only 1.5 percent over the months of 2008.[8] The recapitalization of banks, the fiscal stimulus, and financial regulation reform have all contributed to this increase in consumer confidence in the market.

Despite the fact that the overall trend of the consumer sentiment index in 2009 reflected the signs of an increase in consumer confidence in the market, the Conference Board reported a decline in this index in September and October 2009. Consumers grew pessimistic about current economic conditions and many consumers anticipate that labor market conditions will not improve any time soon. Consumers are also pessimistic about their ability to spend in the coming holiday season. This suggests that it might be somewhat early to expect a lasting improvement in consumer confidence.

[8] Credit spread is the difference between the yield on treasury securities and non-treasury securities that are identical in everything except quality.

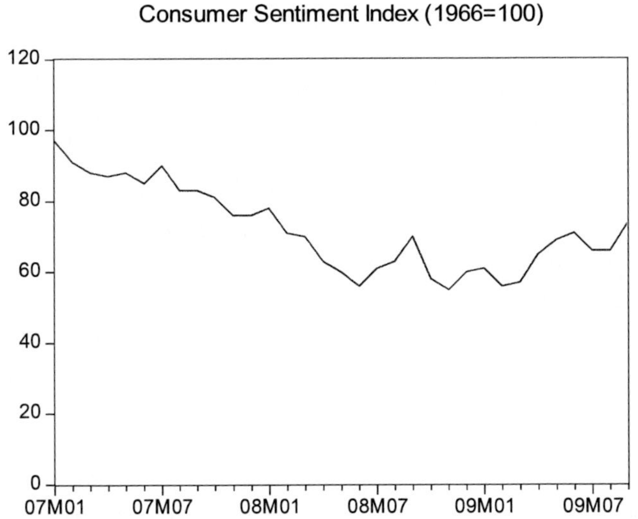

Source: Economic Research, Federal reserve bank of St. Louis http://research.stlouisfed.org/fred2/

Figure 16. Consumer sentiment index (1966=100).

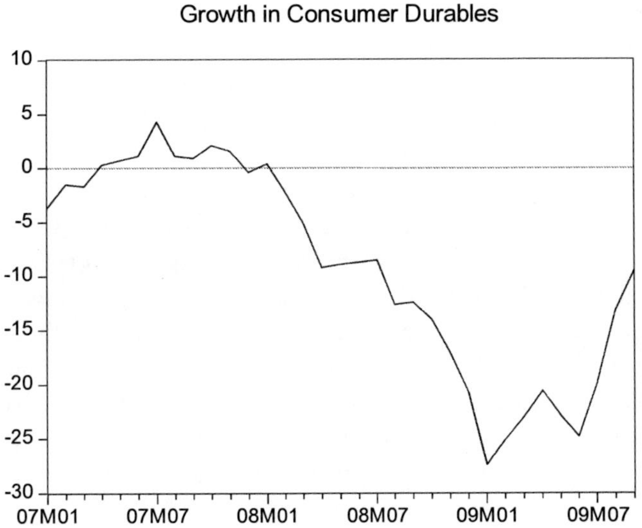

Source: Economic Research, Federal reserve bank of St. Louis, http://research.stlouisfed.org/fred2/

Figure 17. Growth in consumer spending on durable goods.

Closely related to consumer expectation is consumer spending on durable goods. Usually, when consumers expect relatively favorable economic conditions in the future, they allocate a larger portion of their disposable income to the purchase of durable goods. Despite the negative growth in consumer spending on durable goods over all the months of 2008, there has been an upward trend that started in early 2009.

As is made obvious in Figure 17, the growth in consumer spending on durable goods continued to decrease toward the end of 2007, marking negative growth throughout the entirety of 2008. However, by the beginning of 2009 there was an upward trend, with the sharpest jump of about 52 percent from July 2009 to August 2009. One factor explaining this upward trend in consumer spending on durable goods is the $90 billion of economic stimulus delivered by the U.S. federal government in the form of tax rebates to households between May and July 2009. Also, the relative rise in consumer confidence, starting at the beginning of 2009, has contributed to this increase in spending on consumer durables.

Money supply, the third component of the LEI index to be analyzed, is an important indicator of the future increase in aggregate spending in the economy. As the crisis unfolds, with many people losing jobs or facing wage cuts, an increase in money supply would increase consumer spending and increase aggregate spending in turn. The expansion of money supply was required so that money would be available for consumption. As Figure 18 shows, a continuous increase in money supply, adjusted for inflation, began in the summer of 2008 and continued until reaching its peak in May 2009. Despite the fact that there was a slight downward turn of about 1.5 percent from May to August 2009, there was still a considerable jump in money supply right after the onset of the crisis. Using Fisher's quantity theory of money to calculate the velocity of money, theoretical predictions match. During the period in which money supply was increasing, the velocity of money concurred with an opposite change. This decrease in velocity reflects the unwillingness of consumers and businesses to spend the increase in money during that period. This outcome supports the declining behavior of spending on consumer durables. The velocity of money signaled a slight increase only as money supply decreased after May 2009, which also corresponds to an increase in consumer spending on durable goods.

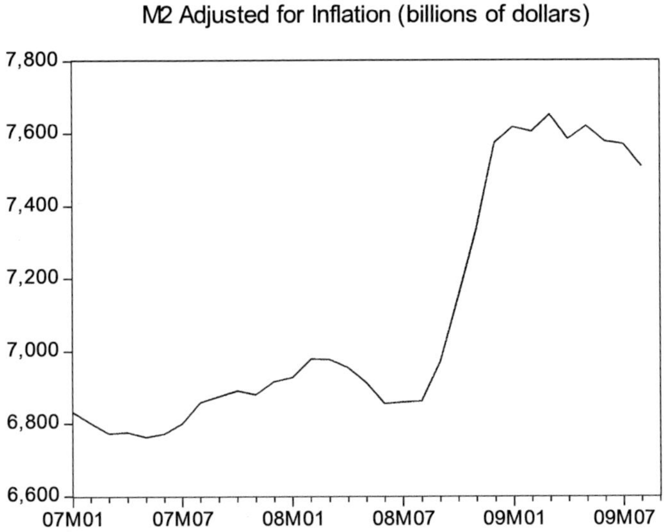

Source: International Financial Statistics database.

Figure 18. M2 Adjusted for inflation in billions of dollars.

Finally, the spread between the ten-year Treasury note and the three-month Treasury bill forms a fourth important component in the computation of the LEI index, reflecting investors' expectations about the market. As the spread increases, or when the yield of the ten-year Treasury note is higher than that of the three-month Treasury bill, it is implied that the economy will expand in the future. In other words, an increase in the spread reflects an expected increase in the interest rate and signifies future economic expansion. Figure 19 shows the movement in the interest rate spread from the beginning of 2007 until September 2009. The figure demonstrates an obvious increase in the average spread, from 0.23 percent in 2007 to 2.3 percent in 2008 to 3 percent in 2009. The introduction of the TAF in mid December 2007 was one factor helping to ease conditions in the interbank market. Other liquidity facilities such as TARP, introduced in October 2008, and TLGP, introduced in November 2008, also contributed to this upward trend in the spread. A study by Christensen (2009) discussed the impact of the liquidity facilities offered by the Fed (such as TAF) on the three-month TED[9] spread, which is measured as the difference between the rates on Libor and the treasury yield. The study finds that the introduction of the TAF and other liquidity facilities contributed positively to the three-month TED spread.

[9] TED stands for Treasury bill and ED, the ticker symbol for the Eurodollar futures contract.

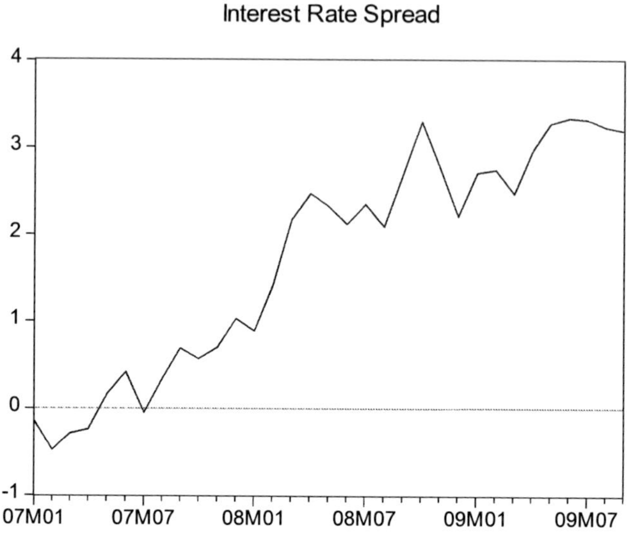

Source: Board of Governors of the Federal Reserve System.

Figure 19. Interest rate spread.

3. Evaluation and Prediction

Based on the above analysis, it can be stated that the complementary actions taken through monetary and fiscal policies to offset the economic recession have proven successful in many ways. The continuous increase in the LEI index from February to August 2009 is an indication that the current recession is about to end. The increase in the growth of the three major U.S. stock indexes is a sign that investors have more confidence in the market. Furthermore, the continuous increase in money supply, starting at the beginning of the crisis, indicates that the level of aggregate spending will increase in the future. This increase will in turn lead to higher levels of output and employment. In addition, the increase in the interest rate spread indicates that investors are optimistic about the future and that they expect future interest rates to rise. Such rises only occur during economic expansions. Finally, the relative increase in the consumer sentiment index from last year to this reflects an improvement in consumer confidence about the market. Despite this fact, confidence is still low compared to its level two years ago. This lower consumer confidence continues to pull the LEI index downward, while consumers remain overloaded with credit card and mortgage debt.

Recovery could also be sluggish at first due to persisting difficulties in certain areas. Based on the 2009 IMF report, U.S. GDP growth is projected to shrink to about 2.8 percent toward the end of 2009 and to a projected zero percent growth toward the end of 2010. These difficulties are reflected in the continuation of tight lending standards by banks to households and firms, the lack of lasting improvement in consumer confidence, the lagging response of unemployment, and the mounting losses faced by many financial institutions.

First, tight standards for lending to households and banks, as reported by the 2009 Senior Loan Officer Opinion Survey on Bank Lending Practices of the Board of Governors, are expected to continue at least until the second half of 2010. The tight lending standards for non-prime households and firms ranked below investment-grade are, however, expected to continue even after the end of 2010.

Second, the lagging response of unemployment is still imposing downward pressure on aggregate spending, with the unemployment rate reaching double digits of 10.2 percent for the first time in 26 years as announced by the November 2009 unemployment report issued by the Labor Department. This lagging response is made worse by the fact that employers continue to cut jobs and reduce the salaries of their current employees.

The third difficulty lies in the non-lasting improvement in consumer confidence. With the increased rate of unemployment, consumers are afraid to spend, and with this reduced spending, the problem of unemployment worsens, and we enter into a vicious circle. According to the conference board, consumer confidence is the one variable that pulled the LEI index downward in September and October 2009. This finding suggests that it might be too early to expect a lasting improvement in consumer confidence.

Finally, U.S. financial institution still face many challenges, including the need to rebuild capital, overcome the continued degrading of their asset values, and slowly discontinuing their dependency on the government for support. The Global Financial Stability Report of the IMF estimated that the total write-downs on U.S.-originated assets since the onset of the crisis in 2007 would reach $2.7 trillion by 2010.

CONCLUSION

The recent financial crisis that has struck the U.S. economy is the worst since the Great Depression. It threatens not only the stability of the financial system, but the economy as a whole. Four main factors have caused the emergence of the recent financial crisis. First, the Fed's remedy package for the 2001 recession was pursued by aggressively lowering interest rates and the ensuing credit boom. Second, the relaxed subprime mortgage markets and the securitization process led to growing leverage in the credit market. The third factor lies in the mismanagement of financial innovation in subprime mortgages and structured credit products. Because of bad management, these products became destructive weapons. The last factor proposed in this chapter is the bursting of the housing bubble with accompanying price declines, defaults, and foreclosures, all leading to the credit crunch.

The outcome of the financial crisis was devastating and rapidly spread throughout the whole economy. Foreclosures, sharp declines in housing prices due to high rates of defaults in subprime mortgages, and the excessive housing supply were signs of the housing market's turmoil. This turmoil created a credit crunch, which squeezed liquidity in the economy. This squeeze in turn caused massive losses and bankruptcies in large financial institutions. These repercussions were reflected in the stock market, in the form of a massive decline in equity values and a significant rise of volatility. The impact of the financial crisis was transmitted to the real economy through a combination of effects: the wealth effect, the confidence effect, the credit channel effect, and the multiplier effect. The combination of these effects ultimately led to declining expenditures on consumption and investment, falling total output, and high rates of unemployment.

Many actions have been taken by the Fed and the U.S. government to restore economic and financial stability. The Fed employed different conventional and unconventional tools to achieve this objective. The set of conventional tools employed included gradual declines in both the federal funds rate and the discount rate, in addition to the provision of short-term liquidity to large financial institutions. Regarding the unconventional approach, the Fed adopted unusual tools related to the direct provision of liquidity to borrowers and investors and those related to the purchase of longer-term securities for the Fed's portfolio. When the tools of monetary policy were deemed insufficient to avert the downward turn of economic activity, a fiscal stimulus was required to complement them. The reactions to the crisis in fiscal policy have been aggressive, with a huge increase in government spending that helped the economy avoid going into another great depression.

The complementary actions taken through monetary and fiscal policies to offset the economic recession have proven successful on many levels and have helped to strengthen investor confidence in the market and restore many of the leading economic indicators. The behaviors of these indicators suggest that the recession has reached its trough already and that there is a good possibility of upcoming growth.

On the other hand, the overall recovery may be sluggish at first due to persisting difficulties in certain areas, leading to negative growth rates of the U.S. GDP. These difficulties include the following: tight standards for lending to firms and households, the lagging response of unemployment that imposes downward pressure on aggregate spending, the non-lasting improvement in consumer confidence that also increases the unemployment problem, and, finally, the enduring challenges facing the U.S. financial institutions, including the need to rebuild capital, overcome the continued degradation of their asset values, and ceasing their dependency on government support.

REFERENCES

Auerbach, A., & Gale, W.. (2009). Activist Policy to Stabilize Economic Activity. Federal Reserve Bank of Kansas City.

Bake, D. (2008). The Housing Bubble and the Financial Crisis. *Real-World Economics Review, 46*, 73–81.

BBC News. (2009). Timeline Credit Crunch to Downturn [online]. http://news.bbc.co.uk/2/hi/business/7521250.stm

Board of Governors of the Federal Reserve System. (2009). Senior Loan Officer Opinion Survey on Bank Lending Practices [online]. http://www.federalreserve.gov/boarddocs/snloansurvey/

Cheng, C. (2007). Global Economic Update: Financial Stress and Macro Outlook [online]. www.econ.ntu.edu.tw/sem-paper/96_1/under_961011.ppt

Chomsisengphet, S. & Pennington-Cross, A. (2006). The Evolution of the Subprime Mortgage Market, *Federal Reserve Bank of St. Louis Review, 88*(1), 31-56.

Christensen, J. (2009). Have the Fed Liquidity Facilities Had an Effect on Libor? FRBSF Working Paper 2009-13 (June).

Christensen, J., Lopez, J. & Rudebusch, G. (2009). Do Central Bank Liquidity Facilities Affect Interbank Lending Rates? FRBSF Working Paper 2009-13 (June). http://www.frbsf.org/publications/economics/papers/2009/wp09-13bk.pdf

Cogan, F., Cwik, T., Taylor, J., & Wieland, V. (2009). New Keynesian versus Old Keynesian Government Spending Multipliers. Unpublished manuscript.

DiMartino, D. & Duca, J. (2007). The Rise and Fall in Subprime Mortgages, *Economic Letter,2(11),* 1-8.

Dowd, K. (2009). Moral Hazard and the Financial Crisis. *Cato Journal, 29*, 141-166

Gilani, S. (2008). Credit default swaps: The Real Reason for the Global Financial Crisis...the Story No One's Talking About [online]. http://www.moneymorning.com/2008/09/18/credit-default-swaps/

Hubbard, G. & O'Brien, A. (2008). Teaching Notes for the Current Financial Crisis. *Macroeconomics* (2nd edition). Upper Saddle River, NJ: Prentice Hall.

International Monetary Fund. (2009). Global Economy Contracts, With Slow Recovery Next Year [online]. *IMF Survey Online.* http://www.imf.org/external/pubs/ft/survey/so/2009/res042209a.htm

International Monetary Fund. (2009). Global Financial Stability Report (GFSR): Executive Summary [online]. https://www.imf.org/external/pubs/ft/gfsr/2009/01/pdf/summary.pdf

Joint Center for Housing Studies of Harvard University. (2008). The State Of The Nation's Housing [online]. Graduate School of Design, Harvard Kennedy School. http://www.jchs.harvard.edu/publications/markets/son2009/index.htm

Kraay, A. & Ventura, J. (2007). The Dot-Com Bubble, the Bush Deficits, and the U.S. Current Account. In *G7 Current Account Imbalances: Sustainability and Adjustment.* Richard Clarida, ed. (457-496). Chicago: University of Chicago Press.

Kwan, S. (2009). Behavior of Libor in the Current Financial Crisis. *FRBSF Economic Letter 2009-04* [online]. http://www.frbsf.org/publications/economics/letter/2009/el2009-04.html

Leduc, S. (2009). Fighting Downturns with Fiscal Policy [online]. *FRBSF Economic Letter 2009-20.* http://www.frbsf.org/publications/economics/letter/2009/el2009-20.html

Levetin, A., Pavlov, A., Fraser, S., & Wachter, S. (2009). Securitization: Cause or Remedy of the Financial Crisis? *Georgetown University Law Center Business, Economics and Regulatory Policy Working Paper Series,* Research Paper No. 1462895.

Mackenzie, S. (2009) The Impact of Financial Crisis on Older Americans. *AARP Public Policy Institute* [online]. http://www.aarp.org/ppi

Makinen, G. (2002) The Economic Effects of 9/11: A Retrospective Assessment [online]. *Report For Congress, Order Code RL31617.* http://www.fas.org/irp/crs/RL31617.pdf

Mankiw, N. (2009). *Macroeconomics* (7th edition). New York: Worth Publishers.

Mishkin, F. (2008). Financial Crisis and the Subprime Meltdown. *The Economics of Money, Banking, and Financial Markets* (8th edition). Upper Saddle River, NJ: Pearson Publishing Company.

Mizen, P. (2008). The Credit Crunch of 2007–2008: A Discussion of the Background, Market Reactions, and Policy Responses. *Federal Reserve Bank of St. Louis Review 90*(5), 531-567.

Mountford,A. & Uhlig, H. (2005). What Are the Effects of Fiscal Policy Shocks? [online]. *SFB 649 Discussion Paper 2005-039.* http://sfb649.wiwi.hu-berlin.de/papers/pdf/SFB649DP2005-039.pdf

NBER. (2008). Determination of the December 2007 Peak in Economic Activity. Version of December 11, 2008.

Otis, L. (2009). Nobel economist Krugman sees slow recovery [online]. http://centraljersey.com/articles/2009/10/27/topstory/doc4ae0d48ceacc1972055746.txt

Reinhart, C. & Rogoff, K. (2008). Is the 2007 U.S. Sub-prime financial crisis so different? An international historical comparison [online]. *NBER, Working Paper 1376.* http://www.nber.org/papers/w13761

Romer, C., & Bernstein, J. (2009). The Job Impact of the American Recovery and Reinvestment Plan. Unpublished manuscript.

Romer, C., & Romer, D. (2008). The Macroeconomic Effects of Tax Changes: Estimates Based on a New Measure of Fiscal Shocks. Unpublished manuscript.

Rosen, Richard. (2007). The role of securitization in mortgage lending. The Federal Reserve Bank of Chicago. Chicago Fed Letter No. 244.

Rudebusch, G. (2009). The Fed's Monetary Policy Response to the Current Crisis [online]. *FRBSF Economic Letter 2009-17.* http://www.frbsf.org/publications/economics/letter/2009/el2009-17.html

Smith, E. (2009). Maybe Unemployment Is Not a Lagging Indicator After All [online]. http://www.businessinsider.com/jobs-arent-coming-back-yet-no-economic-recovery-without-jobs-so-thats-not-good-2009-7

Steil, B. (2009). Lessons of the Financial Crisis [online]. *Council on Foreign Relations, Center for Geoeconomic Studies Council Special Report No. 45.* http://www.cfr.org/publication/18753/lessons_of_the_financial_crisis.html?breadcrumb=%2Fpublication%2Fby_type%2Fspecial_report

Taylor, J. (2008). The Financial Crisis and the Policy Responses: An Empirical Analysis of What Went Wrong [online]. Stanford University working paper. http://www.stanford.edu/~johntayl/FCPR.pdf

The New York Times. (2009). Consumer Borrowing Fall Sharply [online]. The Associated Press. http://www.nytimes.com/2009/11/07/business/economy/07credit.html?_r=1&sq=consumer%20credit&st=nyt&adxnnl=1&scp=11&adxnnlx=1258243277-lY+4Pyl8h7sc8ksXNpKKQQ

Wallison, P. (2008). Everything You Wanted to Know about Credit Default Swaps—but Were Never Told [online], *American Enterprise Institute For Public Policy Research Outlook Series.* http://www.aei.org/outlook/29158

Wood, B. (2009). IMF Predicts Slow Global Recovery from Financial Crisis [online]. http://www.voanews.com/english/archive/2009-04/2009-04-22-voa53.cfmrenderforprint=1&pageid=687030

In: Financial Crisis in the Global ... ISBN: 978-1-61740-597-0
Editors: A. Tomohara, M. Sherlock

Chapter 2

CORPORATE GOVERNANCE AND STOCK PRICE PERFORMANCE DURING THE FINANCIAL CRISIS: EVIDENCE FROM JAPAN

Daisuke Nogata[1], Konari Uchida[2] and Hiroshi Moriyasu[3]
[1]Graduate School of Economics, Kyushu University, Japan
[2]Faculty of Economics, Kyushu University, Japan
[3]Faculty of Economics, Nagasaki University, Japan

ABSTRACT

Previous studies have investigated the argument that corporate governance structures in emerging markets affected firms' stock price performance during the East Asian economic crisis. In this chapter, we analyze how corporate governance structures in an industrial country (Japan) affect firms' stock price performance during the current financial crisis. Results of this study show that Japanese firms that adopt stock option plans have suffered more from deteriorating stock price performance during the present financial crisis. Consistent with Adams (2009), this result suggests that managerial risk-taking incentives induced by stock-based compensations are responsible for declining firm performance during this crisis. Secondly, firms with more non-Japanese shareholders (cross-holding shareholders) experience larger (smaller) stock price reductions. We argue that the Japanese traditional corporate ownership structure stabilizes shareholder valuations of firms. Overall, our results suggest that, for this financial crisis, corporate governance structures are important determinants of firm performance even in industrial countries. Finally, it is apparent that firms that rely on bank financing suffer more from deteriorating stock price performance. Similar to results of existing studies, the results of this study suggest that bank-dependent firms have difficulty in obtaining financing during a financial crisis.

1. Introduction

Bordo and Eichengreen (2002) show that most (95) of the 139 financial crises between 1973 and 1997 occurred in emerging markets. In contrast, the global financial crisis that began in the summer of 2007 originated in the U.S. Consequently, it had a formidable negative impact on industrial countries such as Japan as well as emerging market economies. Severe consumption reductions in the U.S. market during the current financial crisis invariably decreased the earnings of Japanese exporters. The struggle of Japanese companies is symbolized by the fact that Toyota Motor Corp., a Japanese representative automobile manufacturer, fell into a negative operating income situation for the accounting year ending on March 2009: Toyota reported red ink for the first time since the end of the Second World War. The global financial crisis also caused severe stock price declines in Japan: the Tokyo Stock Price Index (TOPIX) fell by 49.6% from August 2007 – December 2008 (see Figure 1).

This chapter investigates what Japanese companies have suffered the most from during the deteriorating stock price performance in the current financial crisis. Given that the current crisis originated in the U.S., it is likely that exporters experience larger losses in shareholder wealth. In addition to the firm's export dependence, we analyze whether corporate governance structures affect the stock price performance. Previous studies have described that in emerging markets corporate governance structures affected stock price performance during the East Asian financial crisis (Baek et al., 2004; Johnson et al., 2000; Mitton, 2002; Lemmon and Lins, 2003). Those studies specifically examined emerging markets because minority shareholders' rights are not well protected in those markets (La Porta, 1998). For the case of the current financial crisis, however, it would be important to analyze how corporate governance structures affect stock returns in industrial countries such as the U.S. and Japan, where minority shareholders' rights are well protected. It is a well-documented idea that banks' executive compensation packages, which are closely linked to bank performance, are a source of U.S. banks' risk-taking behaviors. In addition, Adams (2009) points out that bank boards are at least partly responsible for the crisis. Those views naturally raise the question of whether firms outside the U.S. that adopt stock-based compensation and which have less effective boards have suffered more from deteriorating stock price performance during the current financial crisis.

Existing studies in the literature present the argument that corporate ownership structures in emerging markets are an important factor associated with stock price performance during the East Asian financial crisis. The underlying view of those studies is that the ownership structure determines the degree to which controlling shareholders can expropriate wealth from minor shareholders (Baek et al., 2004; Mitton, 2002; Lemmon and Lins, 2003). In this study, we investigate the effect of ownership structure on stock price performance from a different perspective. We specifically examine how the percentages of ownership by cross-holding shareholders and non-Japanese investors affect the stock price performance. Reports of previous studies have suggested that Japanese cross-shareholdings engender entrenchment effects by releasing incumbent managers from the threat of hostile takeovers, whereas ownership by foreigners is associated with increased firm valuation (Hiraki et al., 2003). During the current financial crisis, however, it is likely that firms that are owned to a greater degree by non-Japanese investors suffer more from deteriorating stock performance because non-Japanese investors are likely to draw their funds from the Japanese stock market. In contrast, firms with more cross-holding shareholders are less likely to suffer from severe stock price declines because those shareholders do not sell stocks substantially, even during a crisis.

Finally, we investigate how firms' financial characteristics affect the stock price performance. Results of previous studies suggest that firms without an alternate financing source (or firms that rely on bank financing) suffer more from deteriorating stock performance during a crisis (Baek et al., 2004; Kang and Stultz, 2000). Japanese companies tend to maintain close relations with the bank; potentially there are firms that rely on bank financing and have no alternate financing sources. Indeed, Kang and Stultz (2000) show evidence that Japanese firms that were more bank-dependent before 1990 experienced significantly larger wealth losses during the first three years of the 1990s, when the Japanese stock market fell dramatically. We analyze whether firms that depend on bank financing suffer more from deteriorating stock price performance during the current financial crisis.

Source. YAHOO Finance Web-site: http://stocks.finance.yahoo.co.jp/

Figure 1. Value of Tokyo Stock Price Index (TOPIX) January 2007 – December 2008).

Several studies have investigated how the current global financial crisis affects corporate financing behaviors (Block and Sandner, 2009; Campello et al., 2009a; 2009b). To the best of our knowledge, however, this chapter is the first to describe how the corporate governance structure affects stock price reductions during the current crisis. As with Adams (2009), the research results augment the literature by analyzing how corporate governance affects firm performance during a crisis in an industrial country.

Our main results are summarized as follows. First, we find evidence that firms adopting stock option plans suffer more from deteriorating stock price performance. Consistent with Adams (2009), this result suggests that incentive pay is responsible for stock price reductions during the current financial crisis. Secondly, firms with more non-Japanese shareholders (cross-holding shareholders) experience larger (smaller) stock price reductions. The result suggests that non-Japanese investors reallocate assets from the Japanese stock market, engendering stock price decreases. In contrast, firms with stable shareholders (cross-holding shareholders) are less susceptible to the global economic crisis. We argue that the Japanese traditional corporate ownership structure (high ownership by cross-holding shareholders and low ownership by foreigners) stabilizes shareholder wealth, whereas previous studies show evidence that the traditional ownership structure is associated with decreased firm value. Overall, regarding the current financial crisis, corporate governance structures are important determinants of stock price performance even in industrial countries. Finally, it is apparent that firms that rely on bank financing suffer more from deteriorating stock price performance, which is consistent with the findings by Kang and Stultz (2000) and Baek et al. (2004).

This chapter is organized as follows. Section 2 presents a survey of relevant studies and develops hypotheses. Section 3 explains the sample and data used in this study. Section 4 shows empirical results. Section 5 is a brief summary of the conclusions of this study.

2. Related Studies and Hypotheses

2.1. Corporate Governance Structures and Stock Price Performance

Previous studies describe analyses of how corporate governance structures affected stock price performance in emerging markets (e.g., Korea, Malaysia, the Philippines, and Thailand) during the East Asian financial crisis of 1997–1998. Johnson et al. (2000) show that country-specific measures of corporate governance have more explanatory power of currency depreciation and stock price reduction than standard macro-economic variables have. Mitton (2002) finds that firms that had higher outside ownership concentration showed better stock price performance in emerging markets during the crisis. Using a sample of 800 firms in eastern Asian countries, Lemmon and Lins (2003) find that crisis-period stock returns are 10–20 percentage points lower for firms in which managers had high levels of control rights, but who had separated their control and cash flow ownership. Baek et al. (2004) show evidence that Korean firms with higher ownership concentration by unaffiliated foreign investors suffered less from deteriorating stock performance during the financial crisis of 1997; in contrast, so-called Chaebol firms—with concentrated ownership by controlling shareholders—experienced a large drop in the value of their equity.

Those studies specifically examined emerging markets because minority shareholders' rights are not well protected in those countries (La Porta et al., 1998). Corporate governance devices serve as an important mechanism by which minority shareholders are protected from expropriation by managers and controlling shareholders.[10] In industrial countries in which minority shareholder rights are well protected, expropriations of minority shareholders will be less severe than in emerging countries. In the case of the current financial crisis that originated in the U.S., however, researchers should devote attention to how corporate governance structures affect the crisis in industrial countries. Indeed, some authors present the argument that weak governance is a cause of the current financial crisis. Adams (2009) points out that the recent resignations of several high-profile financial executives (e.g., Stan O'Neal at Merrill Lynch) and recommendations by several proxy advisors against the reelection of the boards are direct evidence that boards of financial institutions are, at least partly, responsible for the crisis. Additionally, it is well-documented that bankers' compensation packages, which are linked closely to bank performance, give them risk-taking incentives. Adams (2009) shows evidence that banks that received bailout money from the Troubled Assets Relief Program (TARP) have larger boards and greater incentive pay for CEOs.[11] This argument raises a natural question of whether non-financial firms with weak boards and stock-based compensation are more vulnerable to the financial crisis.[12]

From the viewpoint of policymakers, analyses of the effect of corporate governance on firm value have an important meaning. Recently, corporations in both the U.S. and Japan have eagerly conducted corporate governance reforms. It is a well-known assertion that large boards ineffectively monitor management (Lipton and Lorsch, 1992; Jensen, 1993). In according with this notion, U.S. firms decreased their board membership during the 1990s (Linck et al., 2008). More recently, the Sarbanes–Oxley Act of 2002 (Sox) and new exchange listing requirements at the NYSE and Nasdaq have made U.S. firms increase the proportion of independent directors on boards. Similarly, Japanese companies that traditionally had large and insider-dominated boards, substantially downsized their boards recently. Miyajima and Nitta (2006)

---

[10] Mitton (2002) suggests that the role of corporate governance will be more critical during a financial crisis for two reasons: (a) expropriation of minority shareholders might become more severe during a crisis when the expected return on investment falls; (b) a crisis might force investors to recognize and take account of weakness in corporate governance.

[11] The TARP is designed to strengthen the financial system by enabling the government to purchase or insure up to $700 billion in troubled assets. Adams (2009) notes that recipients of TARP money tend to face some financial difficulties, but the U.S. Department of the Treasury does not describe it as a bailout program.

[12] Adams (2009) also finds that firms with TAAP funds have more independent boards. The result is not consistent with the view that bad bank governance practices cause the financial crisis. Adams (2009) interprets the result that independent directors are less likely to have in-depth knowledge of the securitization process.

report that the average number of board members of firms listed on the Tokyo Stock Exchange (TSE) decreased from about 16 in 1995 to 9.8 in 2004. The Japanese Ministry of Economies, Trade, and Industries is considering a mandatory rule that requires firms to adopt at least one outsider on their boards. Many corporate governance researchers analyze the effect of board structure on firm performance and the determinants of board structure (Bennedsen et al., 2008; Boone et al., 2007; Coles et al., 2008; Denis and Sarin, 1999; Eisenberg et al., 1998; Guest, 2008; Lehn et al., 2004; Linck et al., 2008; Mak and Li, 2001; Uchida, 2009a; Yermack, 1996). However, to the best of our knowledge, few works have analyzed how corporate governance mechanisms affect firm value during a crisis (in an industrial country). Given these discussions, we present the following three hypotheses.

- H1: Firms that have large boards experience more deterioration of stock price performance during financial crises.
- H2: Firms that have fewer outsiders on the board experience more deterioration of stock price performance during financial crises.
- H3: Firms that adopt stock option plans experience more deterioration of stock price performance during financial crises.

Given that stock option grants give managers an incentive to maximize shareholder value, we can present a conflicting prediction to H3; that is, firms that adopt stock option plans suffer less from stock price reductions.[13] However, we specifically examine a different aspect of stock option usage. As described earlier, compensation packages that are closely linked to bank performance are likely to be a source of the recent bank crisis (Adams, 2009). In addition, results of recent studies suggest that stock option granting gives managers an incentive for risk-taking (Coles et al., 2006; Cohen et al., 2000; Datta et al., 2001; DeFusco et al., 1990; Guay, 1999). Specifically, DeFusco et al. (1990) suggest that the stock return volatility shows a significant increase after the firm announces stock option grants. Guay (1999) shows evidence that corporate stock return volatility is positively related to the convexity of managerial compensation. Coles et al. (2006) argue that firms in which managerial compensation is more sensitive to the stock return volatility tend to

[13] There are mixed results related to the effect of stock option usage on firm performance in Japan. Kato et al. (2005) report a significantly positive stock price reaction to announcements of stock option usage by Japanese firms. In contrast, Uchida and Matsumoto (2006) find no evidence that firms experience improved operating performance after stock option adoption.

conduct more R&D investments, have more-focused businesses, and have higher leverage. Those findings suggest that firms that use stock option plans will experience more deteriorating performance when the whole economy falls into a more severe downturn. For those reasons, we present H3.

As described, previous studies that specifically examined the East Asian crisis argue that corporate ownership structures are responsible for the degree of stock price reductions during the crisis. We predict that Japanese corporate ownership structures affect firm valuation during the current crisis differently. It is well-documented that cross-shareholdings have been highly developed among Japanese listed companies. Japanese firms formed cross-shareholdings with the intention of blocking potential hostile takeover bids (Morck and Nakamura, 1999; Sheard, 1989); for this reason, cross-holding shareholders have served as stable shareholders. Consequently, Japanese managers tend to care less about shareholder wealth. Bank shareholders have served as a core group of cross-shareholders. Figure 2 shows that, as of 1990, financial institutions held over 40% of the shares of Japanese listed firms. However, the non-performing loan problems that worsened during the late 1990s gave Japanese banks a strong incentive to sell shares. Miyajima and Kuroki (2007) report that banks that had been net buyers of Japanese stocks during 1991–1996 became large net sellers in 1997 and thereafter, when non-performing loan problems worsened. In addition, the Japanese government enacted the Banks' Shareholding Restriction Law in April 2001, which required Japanese banks to decrease shareholdings to the bank's Tier 1 capital level by September 2004 (Uchida, 2009b). As a result, ownership by financial institutions has shown a sharp decline in the last 10 years (Figure 2). Similarly, non-financial firms sold substantial shareholdings probably because large stock-holdings lowered their accounting performance (e.g. ROA). For that reason, cross-shareholdings have shown a substantial decline in the past 15 years. Instead, the percentage of ownership by non-Japanese investors has shown a sharp increase.

Reports of previous studies suggest that ownership structure is an important determinant of Japanese firm value. Hiraki et al. (2003) find that the level of cross-shareholdings is negatively related to Tobin's *Q*, whereas the percentage of ownership by foreigners is positively related to Tobin's *Q*. Morck et al. (2000) argue that Japanese bank shareholders are likely to permit managers to undertake less profitable investments. For that reason, they are associated with lower firm value. Uchida (2009b) argues that firms that have undergone a substantial reduction in the percentage of ownership by banks show improvement in operating performance. In brief, cross-shareholdings (or bank ownership) are likely to decrease shareholder value in normal situations, whereas ownership by foreigners is associated with higher valuation. However, a different tendency is likely to occur during the current financial crisis, which started in the U.S. It is likely that U.S. investors drew their funds from the Japanese stock market, engendering stock price reductions. In contrast, cross-holding shareholders kept their stock holdings even during the crisis and increased stock prices. Those ideas give rise to the following hypotheses.

H4: Firms owned to a greater degree by non-Japanese investors suffer more from deteriorating stock price performance during financial crises.

H5: Firms that have high cross-holding shareholders face less deterioration of stock price performance during financial crises.

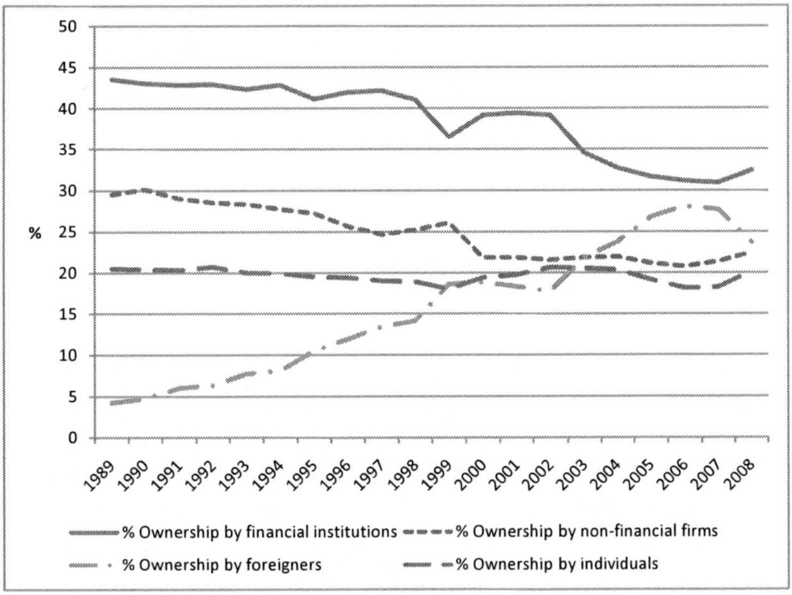

Source: Tokyo Stock Exchange Web-site: http://www.tse.or.jp/

Figure 2. The Japanese corporate ownership structure.
This figure shows the mean percentage of ownership by financial institutions, non-financial institutions shows the mean percentage of ownership by financial institutions, non-financial institutions, individuals, and foreigners for Japanese companies listed on the Tokyo Stock Exchange.

2.2. Corporate Financial Characteristics and Stock Price Performance

It is also be important to analyze how firms' financial characteristics affect firm valuation during the current financial crisis. Ivashina and Scharfstein (2009) document that in the U.S., new loans to large borrowers fell by 47% during the peak period of the financial crisis (fourth quarter of 2008) relative to the prior quarter and by 79% relative to the peak of the credit boom (second quarter of 2007). Given that previous studies show evidence that the corporate investment level is positively related to the firm's liquidity (Fazzari et al., 1988; Hoshi et al., 1991; Whited, 1992), gives rise to the prediction that firms with poor liquidity conditions ecrease investments during a financial crisis. Indeed, Campello et al. (2009a) conducted a survey for 1,050 CFOs in the U.S., Europe, and Asia, and show evidence that the financial crisis strongly affected credit-constrained firms; specifically those firms were forced to cut more planned R&D, employment, and capital spending.[14] Campello et al. (2009b) report that constrained firms draw more funds from their credit lines and that they are more likely to face difficulties in renewing or initiating new lines during a financial crisis.[15] One can infer that firms that have large cash holdings can avoid such problems. This idea gives rise to the following hypothesis.

H6: Firms with poor liquidity status experience more deterioration of stock price performance during financial crises.

Finally, we predict that firms relying more on bank debt suffer more from stock price declines. In general, banks accumulate information about borrowing firms. For that reason, banks can monitor borrowing firms on a less costly basis. If the bank is forced to decrease loans, however, the firm will find it harder to raise funds through other sources (in capital markets) because capital market investors do not have the information that the bank has. Moreover, investors might think that the firm's credit quality is low even when

---

[14] Campello et al. (2009a) show that 86% of constrained U.S. firms said that they had foregone profitable investments during the financial crisis because of difficulties in obtaining external finance. The proportion is about twice as large as that of unconstrained firms that say the same. These numbers are similar in Europe and Asia.

[15] Campello et al. (2009b) also find that the constrained firms have larger credit lines than their large, public, investment-grade, and profitable counterparts both before and during the crisis. This evidence suggests that constrained firms have difficulty raising funds through external financing and therefore optimally use substantial credit lines.

macro-economic conditions force the bank to stop lending to the firm. As a result, the company will be forced to lessen investments and suffer more when banks find it hard to increase the provision of loans. Using Korean firms' data, Baek et al. (2004) show that firms with alternative external financing sources experienced less stock price reduction during the 1997 Korean financial crisis.

Those problems will be evident in Japan, where banks have played an important role in corporate financing and governance. It is well-documented that Japanese companies tend to maintain close ties with their main bank. Previous studies show evidence that Japanese banks exert monopoly power on non-financial firms. Weinstein and Yafeh (1998) report that the debt-to-sales ratio is negatively associated with firms' accounting performance. Pinkowitz and Williamson (2001) show evidence that Japanese banks require firms to have large cash holdings. Those findings suggest that, in Japan, some firms have no alternate financing sources and must rely on bank borrowing. Hoshi et al. (1991) suggest that close relations with banks help Japanese companies avoid liquidity constraints. Hoshi et al. (1990) show evidence that firms affiliated with a keiretsu group decrease sales and fixed investments less after they encounter financial distress.[16] Those results suggest that Japanese firms will face severe liquidity constraints and increased bankruptcy costs if a financial crisis forces banks to decrease lending. Consistent with this idea, Kang and Stultz (2000) find that firms that were more bank-dependent before 1990 experienced significantly larger wealth losses during the first three years of the 1990s, during which the Japanese stock market fell dramatically.[17] We investigate whether the same tendency is apparent during the current financial crisis (H7).

H7: Firms that rely more on bank debt experience more deterioration in stock price performance during financial crises.

3. Sample and Data

Following Ivashina and Scharfstein (2009), we define the financial crisis period as August 2007 – December 2008. The financial crisis period is divided

[16] Recent studies show that financial assistance is provided even to companies that should be shut down instead (Hoshi and Kashyap, 2004; Peek and Rosengren, 2005).

[17] Kang and Stultz (2000) report that the stock return of a firm with no bank loans exceeded the stock return of a firm with only bank loan financing by about 26%, keeping all other firm characteristics unchanged.

into two subperiods and the stock performance measures are calculated for the entire crisis period and for the subperiods. Hereinafter, we use the following notation: *Crisis 1* (August 2007 – July 2008); *Crisis 2* (August 2008 – December 2008); *Crisis 3* (August 2007 – December 2008). *Crisis 1* starts with the collapse of the subprime market in the summer of 2007. Crisis 2 begins in the month when the credit default swap (CDS) spreads of financial institutions start rising. It then covers the period of greatest concern in the liquidity and solvency of the financial system (Ivashina and Scharfstein, 2009). *Crisis 3* represents the entire crisis period.

We use the buy-and-hold return (BHR) during the financial crisis as a proxy for the stock price performance. It is computed using the following equation.

$$BHR_{ic} = \prod_{t=BDc}^{EDc}(1+r_{it})-1$$

Table 1. Definitions of variables

Variable	Definition
BHR	Buy-and hold stock return during the financial crisis
BOARDSIZE	Number of board members
OUTDIR	Percentage of outsiders among board members
SOPD	Stock option dummy: 1 for firms that adopt stock option plans; zero for firms not using stock options
DIRECOWN	Percentage ownership by directors
FOREOWN	Percentage ownership by non-Japanese investors
CROSSOWN	Percentage ownership by cross-holding shareholders
CASH	Cash divided by assets
BANKD	Borrowings divided by assets
BOND	Bonds and commercial papers divided by assets
Beta	Market beta of the stock
Past stock return	Buy-and hold stock return for 6 months preceding the crisis peri
Ln_MVALUE	Natural logarithm of market value of common stocks
PBR	Price-to-book ratio
EXPORT	Export sales divided by sales

In that equation, subscript $c=1,2,3$ respectively represent the crisis periods (*Crisis 1*, *Crisis 2*, and *Crisis 3*) and r_{it} is the stock return of firm i for day t. In addition, BD_c and ED_c respectively represent the beginning and ending days of Crisis c.

Corporate board structure data are available from *Nikkei NEEDS Cges*. BOARDSIZE is the number of board members and OUTDIR represents the percentage of outsiders among board members (see Table 1 for the definition of variables). We define the stock option dummy (SOPD) as the dummy variable which takes a value of one for firms that use stock option plans and zero for others. Corporate ownership structure data comes from *Nikkei NEEDS FinancialQuest* and *Nikkei NEEDS Cges*: percentage ownership by foreigners (FOREOWN) and percentage ownership by cross-holding shareholders (CROSSOWN). Corporate financial data are also available from *Nikkei NEEDS FinancialQuest.* As a liquidity measure, we adopt cash divided by assets (CASH). We adopt short-term and long-term borrowing divided by assets (BANKD) as a proxy for the degree to which the firm relies on bank financing. For each crisis period, the sample consists of Japanese firms that are listed on the Tokyo Stock Exchange for which stock price data and variables described above are available. Banks and insurance companies are deleted from the analysis because the financial statement format differs from that of non-financial firms.

Table 2 shows descriptive statistics, which suggest that the average sample firm lost 43% of its shareholder value during the entire crisis period (Crisis *3*). Given that *Crisis 2* is only a 5-month period and the fact that the reported BHR_2 is almost identical to BHR_1 suggests that Japanese firms experienced tremendous stock price reductions, especially during *Crisis 2*. Apart from BHR, Table 2 reports *Crisis 3* data. The average corporate board includes 9.2 members. As a result of recent corporate board downsizing, the mean board size in Japan has become similar to that of U.S. firms (Miyajima and Nitta, 2006; Uchida, 2009a). In contrast, appointments of outsiders to the board are still less common in Japan: the median OUTDIR is zero and the mean is only 8.6%. As a result of the unwinding of cross-shareholdings that started in the late 1990s, the mean CROSSOWN is only 8.7%. Instead, the percentage of ownership by non-Japanese investors has recently increased: the mean FOREOWN is about 12.6%, which is substantially higher than CROSSOWN. It is commonly viewed that traditional Japanese companies rely on bank financing. For the average sample firm, bank debt accounts for about 15% of assets.

Table 2. Descriptive statistics

Buy-and-hold return for each crisis period				
BHR_1	-0.240	0.259	-0.245	1988
BHR_2	-0.266	0.230	-0.264	1952
BHR_3	-0.427	0.289	-0.460	1964
Descriptive statistics of variables for Crisis 3				
BOARDSIZE	9.175	3.720	8	1964
OUTDIR	0.086	0.130	0	1964
SOPD	0.330	0.470	0	1964
DIRECOWN	0.052	0.096	0.007	1964
FOREOWN	0.126	0.119	0.095	1964
CROSSOWN	0.087	0.087	0.065	1964
CASH	0.101	0.100	0.073	1964
BANKD	0.154	0.159	0.105	1964
BOND	0.029	0.059	0	1964
BETA	0.785	0.381	0.797	1944
Past stock return	0.004	0.249	-0.030	1944
ROE	0.039	0.336	0.057	1963
Ln_MVALUE	10.756	1.624	10.494	1964
PBR	1.686	1.320	1.337	1964
EXPORT	0.061	0.151	0	1964

4. Empirical Results

4.1. Mean Buy-and-Hold Return during the Financial Crisis

To test the presented hypotheses, we divide sample firms into groups based on the variables described in Section 3 and compare the mean BHR across groups. Principally, the sample firms are divided equally into 10 groups. For stock option usage, we divide sample firms into two groups (firms that adopt stock option plans (Group 1) and others (Group 2)). Regarding variables that take a value of zero for many companies (EXPORT; CROSSOWN; BANKD), we make a group comprising firms for which the variable takes a value of zero, and equally divide the remaining firms so that each group has about 160–200 observations. As a result, we form fewer than 10 groups for EXPORT. Regarding the variables for which many firms take the same value (BOARDSIZE and OUTDIR), we allow each group to have a different number of observations.[18] We relate corporate financial data for the accounting year ending during August 2006 – July 2007 to BHR_1 and BHR_3; financial data for accounting years ending during August 2007 – July 2008 are used for analysis of BHR_2.

Results are presented in Table 3. First, the highest EXPORT group (Group 1) reports mean BHR_1 of -31%. The figure is much worse than that of Group 4 (firms with zero export sales) and Group 3 (the lowest EXPORT group among firms with non-zero EXPORT). The negative effect of EXPORT on BHR is more evident during *Crisis 2*. Group 1 firms report mean BHR_2 of -40%, which is significantly and economically worse than the Group 4 BHR_2 (-25%). Consequently, the mean BHR_3 decreases almost monotonically with EXPORT. This finding is consistent with the view that the recent financial crisis severely damaged Japanese exporters.

Hypotheses H1 and H2 specifically address the relationship between corporate board structure and the stock price performance. Regarding BOARDSIZE, Groups 1–3 (the three highest BOARDSIZE groups) suffer less from stock price reductions during *Crisis 1* than Groups 6–8 (the three lowest BOARDSIZE groups). In addition, Group 1 firms experience the smallest losses in shareholder value during *Crisis 2*. Those figures are not consistent with the notion that firms that have large boards experienced more stock performance deterioration during the financial crisis (H1). Group 5 for OUTDIR (firms that have no outside directors) has lower stock price performance than other groups do during *Crisis 1* (and a significant mean difference exists between Group 1 and Group 5). However, Group 1 (the highest OUTDIR group) reports the worst stock performance during *Crisis 2*; it is significantly lower than the Group 5 mean. Our data do not present strong evidence that corporate boards that have more outsiders functioned well during the crisis.

[18] Many sample firms have boards of 9 or 11 members including one outsider.

Table 3. Financial characteristics and buy-and-hold return during the financial crisis

This table shows mean and median buy-and-hold returns of Japanese stocks during the financial crisis. Sample companies are Japanese firms listed on the Tokyo Stock Exchange for which stock price data and necessary variables are available. Sample companies are divided into groups based on the variables that potentially affect stock price performance in the following way. Principally, the sample firms are equally divided into 10 groups based on the variable. For SOPD, we divide the sample firms into two groups (firms that use stock options (Group 1) and those that do not use stock options (Group 2). For variables that take a value of zero for many companies, we make a group that consists of zero observations and divide the remaining firms so that each group has 160--200 firms (EXPORT; CROSSOWN; BANKD). For variables for which many firms take a same value, we allow each group to have a different number of firms (BOARDSIZE; OUTDIR). We calculate firms' buy-and-hold returns during the financial crisis and show the mean and median returns by each of the groups. In addition, *t*-statistics are for the null hypothesis that the mean BHR is identical between the highest (Group 1) and lowest groups. See Table 1 for definitions of variables.

Group		1 (High)	2	3	4	5	6	7	8	9	10 (Low)	*t*-statistics
Panel A: Crisis 1 (August 2007 -- July 2008)												
EXPORT	Mean (%)	-31.2	-26.0	-19.4	-23.4							-4.05 ***
	N	187	186	185	1430							
BOARDSIZE	Mean (%)	-20.0	-21.9	-21.7	-25.3	-22.7	-24.2	-29.0	-27.5			3.26 ***
	N	232	328	176	238	270	270	228	246			
OUTDIR	Mean (%)	-21.4	-23.7	-23.3	-21.3	-25.1						2.06 **
	N	204	186	217	217	1164						
SOPD	Mean (%)	-26.2	-22.9									-2.67 ***
	N	659	1329									
FOREOWN	Mean (%)	-25.9	-26.3	-29.0	-25.7	-23.3	-23.5	-24.6	-22.9	-18.1	-20.6	-2.45 ***
	N	199	199	199	199	198	199	199	199	199	198	
CROSSOWN	Mean (%)	-22.1	-23.0	-20.2	-24.3	-23.5	-21.6	-22.5	-23.1	-28.6	-28.2	2.32 **
	N	188	186	186	186	186	186	188	184	185	313	

CASH	Mean (%)	-25.8	-21.2	-27.3	-27.8	-24.5	-27.6	-23.7	-23.7	-18.1	-20.3	-2.31	**
	N	199	199	199	199	198	199	199	199	199	198		
BANKD	Mean (%)	-30.2	-25.1	-25.0	-24.1	-25.2	-27.0	-20.4	-22.9	-21.0	-21.8	-3.63	***
	N	178	175	176	175	176	175	176	175	175	407		
Panel B: Crisis 2 (August 2008 -- December 2008)													
EXPORT	Mean (%)	-40.1	-34.1	-21.7	-24.8							-8.18	***
	N	167	166	166	1453								
BOARDSIZE	Mean (%)	-23.5	-26.2	-26.9	-26.6	-25.5	-27.6	-26.9	-29.4			2.40	***
	N	211	313	184	236	238	295	231	244				
OUTDIR	Mean (%)	-31.3	-27.5	-25.5	-24.4	-26.4						-2.63	***
	N	181	239	169	270	1093							
SOPD	Mean (%)	-28.2	-25.8									-2.17	**
	N	645	1307										
FOREOWN	Mean (%)	-37.1	-29.1	-31.3	-29.9	-23.9	-24.2	-23.3	-22.4	-23.3	-21.8	-7.29	***
	N	196	195	195	195	195	196	195	195	195	195		
CROSSOWN	Mean (%)	-22.1	-26.9	-27.2	-24.0	-27.3	-26.8	-26.1	-23.4	-30.4	-29.6	3.45	***
	N	183	182	182	181	180	181	181	181	181	320		
CASH	Mean (%)	-20.8	-26.2	-27.1	-26.2	-25.4	-27.9	-26.5	-31.3	-29.6	-25.2	1.79	*
	N	196	195	195	195	195	196	195	195	195	195		
BANKD	Mean (%)	-29.3	-29.1	-29.6	-29.3	-30.3	-27.1	-26.3	-26.1	-22.0	-22.4	-3.13	***
	N	175	172	173	172	173	172	173	172	172	398		

Table 3. Continued

Panel C: Crisis 3 (August 2007 -- December 2008)													
EXPORT	Mean (%)	-59.2	-50.6	-36.7	-40.2							-8.80	***
	N	186	185	185	1408								
BOARDSIZE	Mean (%)	-38.4	-40.7	-42.9	-43.3	-40.5	-43.8	-44.9	-47.6			3.49	***
	N	232	325	175	233	268	265	222	244				
OUTDIR	Mean (%)	-44.2	-42.5	-41.8	-38.8	-43.3						-0.41	
	N	202	182	213	214	1153							
SOPD	Mean (%)	-44.8	-41.6									-2.33	***
	N	648	1316										
FOREOWN	Mean (%)	-50.9	-46.9	-48.6	-45.2	-41.2	-41.4	-42.1	-39.0	-35.3	-35.9	-5.96	***
	N	197	196	197	196	196	197	196	197	196	196		
CROSSOWN	Mean (%)	-39.6	-43.0	-40.4	-41.7	-42.1	-41.6	-41.6	-42.6	-46.4	-45.7	2.17	**
	N	186	184	184	184	185	183	184	184	184	306		
CASH	Mean (%)	-42.6	-38.3	-43.4	-45.3	-43.6	-45.7	-43.3	-43.2	-41.5	-39.8	-1.00	
	N	197	196	197	196	196	197	196	197	196	196		
BANKD	Mean (%)	-47.0	-45.9	-42.1	-46.8	-46.8	-44.5	-40.9	-42.2	-38.7	-37.9	-3.42	***
	N	175	174	173	173	173	174	173	173	173	403		

***: Significant at the 1% level

**: Significant at the 5% level

*: Significant at the 10% level

Table 4. Portfolio returns

This table shows returns of portfolios that consist of firms that are similar in a specific variable. Sample companies are Japanese firms listed on the Tokyo Stock Exchange for which stock price data and necessary variables are available. Sample companies are divided into some groups based on variables that potentially affect stock price performance in the following way. Principally, the sample firms are equally divided into 10 groups based on the variables. For SOPD, we divide the sample firms into two groups (firms that use stock options (Group 1) and those that do not use stock options (Group 2). For variables that take a value of zero for many companies, we make a group that consists of zero observations and divide the remaining firms so that each group has 160--200 firms (EXPORT; CROSSOWN; BANKD). For variables for which many firms take a same value, we allow each group to have a different number of firms (BOARDSIZE; OUTDIR). We produce portfolios that consist of companies belonging to a same group and compute value-weighted returns of the portfolios during the financial crisis. See Table 1 for definitions of variables.

Group	1 (High)	2	3	4	5	6	7	8	9	10 (Low)
					(%)					
Panel A: Crisis 1 (August 2007 -- July 2008)										
EXPORT	-28.4	-23.7	-15.5	-18.6						
BOARDSIZE	-22.0	-18.2	-24.1	-27.2	-27.0	-24.4	-26.0	-13.9		
OUTDIR	-21.0	-21.8	-15.7	-16.8	-25.5					
SOPD	-25.2	-19.1								
FOREOWN	-22.3	-24.4	-22.3	-14.9	-22.5	-17.8	-18.7	-16.2	-11.6	-15.2
CROSSOWN	-19.7	-21.1	-26.7	-21.7	-23.1	-19.4	-21.5	-20.1	-24.4	-14.8
CASH	-19.9	-15.1	-23.6	-22.2	-23.5	-18.6	-29.5	-21.9	-25.6	-16.0
BANKD	-33.6	-22.9	-21.4	-20.7	-19.9	-24.4	-21.3	-20.1	-20.7	-20.7

Table 4. Continued

Panel B: Crisis 2 (August 2008 -- December 2008)										
EXPORT	-42.2	-38.0	-15.5	-28.0						
BOARDSIZE	-31.0	-30.9	-40.0	-36.6	-29.7	-31.8	-26.0	-17.1		
OUTDIR	-41.9	-31.6	-18.9	-26.3	-32.9					
SOPD	-37.2	-26.7								
FOREOWN	-37.8	-34.7	-29.6	-18.5	-17.5	-17.8	-11.6	-16.6	-14.6	-13.8
CROSSOWN	-35.1	-42.8	-34.9	-28.4	-35.1	-33.3	-23.2	-31.7	-39.2	-14.2
CASH	-24.0	-23.6	-36.8	-33.3	-28.3	-19.7	-33.5	-42.3	-33.6	-30.0
BANKD	-32.4	-35.1	-38.0	-27.5	-33.2	-24.4	-35.3	-32.1	-36.7	-29.8
Panel C: Crisis 3 (August 2007 -- December 2008)										
EXPORT	-58.6	-52.4	-30.4	-40.9						
BOARDSIZE	-46.9	-43.5	-54.2	-52.7	-48.6	-49.4	-41.9	-27.1		
OUTDIR	-52.0	-49.4	-31.5	-39.2	-50.1					
SOPD	-53.2	-41.2								
FOREOWN	-51.1	-51.6	-44.6	-30.1	-38.9	-34.3	-32.1	-30.4	-21.4	-26.7
CROSSOWN	-41.0	-55.1	-51.7	-47.4	-49.7	-44.3	-43.1	-43.3	-49.8	-30.8
CASH	-43.1	-36.4	-47.2	-50.3	-50.5	-36.2	-56.3	-50.9	-53.2	-37.3
BANKD	-58.3	-50.1	-51.8	-41.7	-41.8	-46.0	-45.2	-47.0	-50.1	-43.5

Hypothesis H3 would be validated if stock option adoptions induce managerial risk-taking incentives and lower the stock price performance during the crisis. Consistent with this hypothesis, Table 3 suggests that firms that adopt stock option plans suffer more from deteriorating performance, irrespective of the crisis period.

Our hypotheses H4–H5 specifically relate to the effect of ownership structures on the stock price performance during the financial crisis. As described, previous studies suggest a positive relationship between the ownership by non-Japanese investors and firm value. However, results presented in Table 3 suggest that firms that are owned less by non-Japanese investors experience smaller stock price reductions during the financial crisis. The two lowest FOREOWN groups (Groups 9 and 10) show the mean BHR_1 of about -20% or better. In contrast, the four highest FOREOWN groups (Groups 1–4) have mean BHR_1 of about -25% or worse. During *Crisis 2*, Groups 1–4 lose approximately 30% or more shareholder wealth, whereas Groups 7–10 report mean BHR_2 of -21% to -23%. Results show that the stock performance for the entire crisis period (BHR_3) decreases almost monotonically with FOREOWN, suggesting that high percentage of ownership by foreigners aggravated the stock price reduction during the financial crisis (H4). Regarding CROSSOWN, the lowest two groups (Groups 9 and 10) report worse mean BHR_1 than most other groups. During *Crisis 2*, the highest CROSSOWN group (Group 1) shows a mean BHR_2 of about -22%, whereas many of Groups 2–7 report a mean BHR_2 of about -27%. Importantly, Group 10 (firms that have no cross-holding shareholders) report -30% BHR_2 on average, which is significantly worse than the Group 1 mean. During the entire crisis period, the highest CROSSOWN group (Group 1) lost less than 40% of shareholder value, whereas shareholders of Groups 9 and 10 firms lost 45% or more of their value. Consistent with H5, those figures suggest that stable shareholders mitigate stock price declines during the financial crisis.

Hypothesis H6 would be supported if cash-rich firms suffered less from stock price reductions. However, the highest CASH group (Group 1) has a worse BHR_1 and BHR_3 than the lowest group (Group 10) has; especially, the BHR_1 mean difference is statistically significant. The univariate test reveals no clear tendency of BHR increasing with CASH. We also conduct analyses that use cash and marketable securities or cash flow (divided by assets) instead of CASH; the additional analyses do not find a clear positive relationship between BHR and those liquidity measures.

Finally, H7 would be supported if firms that rely on bank borrowing were likely to suffer from deteriorating stock price performance. Looking at

BANKD groups, the highest group (Group 1) reports the mean BHR_1 of -30%, but it increases to approximately -21% for Groups 7–10. Those results suggest that BHR_1 decreases almost monotonically with BANKD. During *Crisis 2*, Groups 1–5 report mean BHR_2 of about -30%; it increases to about -22% for Groups 9–10. A similar tendency is observed for the whole crisis period (*Crisis 3*); a significant mean BHR_3 difference exists between Group 1 and Group 10. Those findings are consistent with H7.

4.2. Portfolio Returns

In the former section, we showed evidence that EXPORT, SOPD, FOREOWN, CROSSOWN, and BANKD are associated with stock price reduction during the financial crisis. As an additional test, we compute returns of portfolios that consist of companies that are similar in terms of the variables suggested in Section 3. Specifically, we produce portfolios consisting of companies belonging to the same group (defined in the previous section) and compute the value-weighted returns of the portfolios. The analysis is an attempt to examine whether investors avoid large losses during the financial crisis by adopting a specific investment strategy.

Results are presented in Table 4. Consistent with H3, the strategy that invests in firms that adopt stock option plans brings larger losses than investments in non-stock option adopting firms. The former strategy experiences 12% higher losses during the entire crisis period than the latter. This result provides support for H3. Consistent with H4, all period results show clear evidence that investment strategies that buy stocks of firms with low percentage ownerships by non-Japanese investors can avoid large losses during the crisis. The entire period result suggests that investment strategies that buy bank-dependent firms' shares have larger losses than those that invest in less bank-dependent companies. For example, investors who invest in the BANKD Group 1 lose 58% of their share values during the entire crisis period, whereas those who invest in firms with no bank debt (BANKD Group 10) experience 43.5% decline in their share values. These results are consistent with H7.

Differently from the former results, Table 4 shows no clear tendency by which investments in portfolios that consist of firms with more cross-holding shareholders avoid large drops in wealth. For the entire crisis period, the CROSSOWN Group 1 portfolio loses 41% of their value, which is worse than the return of the portfolio made by firms with no cross-holding shareholders (-

31%). Given that the value-weighted return is sensitive to large-stocks' returns, a possible interpretation of the result is that large companies suffer less from deteriorating stock performance even if the percentage of ownership by cross-holding shareholders is low.

As with the former result, Table 4 shows no clear evidence that investment strategies that buy shares of firms that have small boards with outsiders can avoid tremendous losses during the financial crisis. Regarding CASH, the *Crisis 1* and *Crisis 3* results show that the Group 1 portfolio return is worse than that of Group 10. As is true for the former result, no clear evidence supports H6.

4.3. Regression of BHR

In this section, we conduct regressions of BHR to evaluate whether each variable has a significant impact on BHR when controlling for other variables' effects. Results are presented in Table 5. Following the Fama and French (1993) and Carhart (1997) four factor model, we include market beta (BETA), the natural logarithm of the market value of common stocks (Ln_MVALUE), and the price-to-book ratio (PBR), along with past stock returns in independent variables. For the *Crisis 1* and *Crisis 3* analyses (*Crisis 2* analysis), the BETA and past stock return values are calculated using 6-month stock price data of February 2007 – July 2007 (February 2008 – July 2008). All estimations include industry dummy variables (results not reported). The observations are fewer than those used in the former (univariate) analysis because of the availability of additional control variables.

Results are presented in Table 5. Of the corporate governance variables, SOPD has a negative and significant coefficient in the *Crisis 1* and *Crisis 3* regressions. Together with the former result, this result suggests that firms using stock option plans as compensation packages suffer more from deteriorating stock performance (H3). Recently Japanese companies have increasingly adopted stock option plans as a managerial compensation package (Kato et al., 2005; Uchida, 2006). However, high-risk strategies induced by stock option grants worsen stock price performance during the financial crisis; the result highlights the dark side of stock-based compensations. Our finding is also consistent with evidence from Adams (2009) showing that banks with TARP funds have greater incentive pay for CEOs.

Table 5. Regression reseults

This table presents regression results of the buy-and-hold return during the financial crisis. Sample firms are Japanese companies listed on the Tokyo Stock Exchange for which stock price data and necessary data are available. BHR_1, BHR_2, and BHR_3 respectively represent the buy-and-hold return during the *Crisis 1* (August 2007 -- July 2008), *Crisis 2* (August 2008 -- December 2008), and *Crisis 3* (August 2007 -- December 2008). For the independent variable, data of accounting year that ends from August 2006 to July 2007 (August 2007 -- July 2008) are used for the BHR_1 and BHR_3 regressions (BHR_2 regression). Figures in parentheses are *t*-statistics computed using robust standard errors. See Table 1 for definitions of variables.

	Crisis 1	*Crisis 2*	*Crisis 3*
Dependent variable	BHR_1	BHR_2	BHR_3
BOARDSIZE	0.003 *	0.002	0.004 **
	(1.76)	(1.26)	(1.98)
OUTDIR	0.066	-0.044	-0.026
	(-1.39)	(-1.18)	(-0.53)
SOPD	-0.026 **	-0.010	-0.025 **
	(-2.14)	(-0.94)	(-2.01)
FOREOWN	-0.204 ***	-0.338 ***	-0.425 ***
	(-3.20)	(-5.63)	(-6.33)
CROSSOWN	0.091	0.166 ***	0.156 ***
	(1.51)	(3.30)	(2.39)
DIRECOWN	-0.166 **	0.095	-0.078
	(-2.27)	(1.45)	(-0.96)
CASH	-0.047	0.078	-0.015
	(-0.68)	(1.28)	(-0.22)
BANKD	-0.096 **	-0.205 ***	-0.197 ***
	(-2.05)	(-5.33)	(-3.96)
BOND	0.151	-0.115	0.013
	(1.34)	(-1.07)	(0.12)
EXPORT	-0.124 ***	-0.122 ***	-0.189 ***
	(-3.20)	(-4.05)	(-5.82)
BETA	-0.031 *	-0.084 ***	-0.086 ***
	(-1.74)	(-5.25)	(-4.70)
Ln_MVALUE	0.012 *	0.022 ***	0.025 ***
	(1.76)	(4.31)	(3.28)
PBR	0.002	-0.003	0.007
	(0.21)	(-0.73)	(0.62)
Past stock return	-0.021	0.026	-0.080 ***
	(-0.73)	(1.22)	(-3.43)
ROE	-0.014	-0.010	-0.025 *
	(-1.19)	(-1.19)	(-1.81)
Constant	-0.293 ***	-0.356 ***	-0.525 ***
	(-4.67)	(-7.61)	(-7.60)
Industry dummy		Yes	
adj. $R2$	0.168	0.294	0.291
N	1967	1932	1943

***: Significant at the 1% level

**: Significant at the 5% level

*: Significant at the 10% level

In contrast, the regression result does not carry a positive coefficient on OUTDIR. It is particularly interesting that BOARDSIZE has a positive coefficient and that it is statistically significant in the entire crisis regression (at the 5% level); the presented result contradicts the notion that large boards do not function well because of free-rider problems (Lipton and Lorsch, 1992; Jensen, 1993). As described, recently Japanese companies have conducted board reforms (board downsizing and adoption of outsiders on the board). However, our results do not show evidence that the board reform contributes to avoidance of large losses during a financial crisis. This finding is consistent with recent empirical studies which argue that small and outsider-dominated boards do not necessarily contribute to increased shareholder value (Boone et al., 2007; Coles et al., 2008; Guest, 2008; Lehn et al., 2004; Linck et al., 2008; Uchida, 2009a).

Irrespective of the analytical period, FOREOWN has a negative and significant coefficient; the result is consistent with the view that the financial crisis compelled U.S. investors to exit from the Japanese stock market, engendering stock price reductions (H4). It sharply contrasts with the finding of Baek et al. (2004) that Korean firms owned more by unaffiliated foreign investors suffered less from deteriorating shareholder values during the East Asian crisis. Differently from the East Asian crisis, the current financial crisis caused U.S. investors' exit from the non-U.S. stock market; they do not play a role of mitigating expropriation of minority shareholders. Consistent with H5, CROSSOWN has positive coefficients; *Crisis 2* and *Crisis 3* coefficients are statistically significant. Firms that have more stable shareholders suffer less from stock price declines during financial crises. Those results contradict the view that cross-shareholdings make managers care less about shareholder wealth, whereas ownership by foreigners is related to increased firm value; the relation is opposite during the crisis. We interpret that the traditional Japanese corporate ownership structure—with ownership mainly by cross-holding shareholders, with less by foreigners—makes shareholder wealth less volatile. In addition to FOREOWN and CROSSOWN, we include DIRECOWN (percentage of ownership by directors) among the independent variables because many corporate governance studies show evidence that insider ownership is positively related to firm value at certain ownership levels (McConnell and Servaes, 1990, 1995; Morck et al., 1988). For the case of Japan, Chen et al. (2003) and Hiraki et al. (2003) show evidence that firm value increases monotonically with the percentage of ownership by directors. However, no evidence suggests that managerial ownership contributes to smaller losses in shareholder value during a financial crisis. Rather, the managerial ownership shows a negative and significant impact on BHR during *Crisis 1*.

As with the univariate test results, all regression results carry negative and significant coefficients on BANKD. Consistent with results by Baek et al. (2004) and Kang and Stultz (2000), shareholders of firms that rely more on bank financing suffer more during a nationwide economic downturn. Those companies have no alternative financing sources. Consequently, they are highly vulnerable to banks' struggles. It is also likely that the bankruptcy costs of those firms increase during periods when banks face severe conditions. An important caveat is that the negative coefficient on BANKD might simply represent leverage effects because we measure firms' bank dependence by the proportion of bank debt over assets. In fact, BANKD might be positively correlated with the debt ratio. We include the ratio of bond and commercial paper to assets (BOND) to test that possibility. Table 5 shows that BOND has no significant coefficient in any estimation, suggesting that the negative BANKD coefficient does not come from leverage effects. Another caveat is that the analysis does not fully control for the endogeneity of BANKD; it is likely that weak companies tend to rely on bank financing and that those companies suffer more during an economic crisis (Kang and Stultz, 2000). We include return on equity (ROE; net income divided by assets less total liabilities) to address this concern. Results show that ROE has negative coefficients; our data does not support the view that poorly performing firms rely on bank debt and experience large stock price reductions during a financial crisis. Finally, Table 5 shows that the *Crisis 2* regression engenders an economically larger (in the negative direction) coefficient on BANKD. This result is consistent with Ivashina and Scharfstein (2009), who found that a harsher credit-crunch occurred during *Crisis 2*.[1]

As with the univariate analysis, no estimation carries a significant coefficient on CASH. Our data does not support the notion that firms that have large cash holdings suffer less from deteriorating stock performance (H6). We also conduct regression analyses that uses cash flow or cash and marketable securities (divided by assets) instead of CASH; the result is qualitatively unchanged. A possible interpretation of the result is that firms that have low cash holdings draw funds from credit lines (Campello et al., 2009b).

Regarding other variables, EXPORT has a negative and significant coefficient irrespective of the crisis period. Consistent with the well-

[1] Ivashina and Scharfstein (2009) show that in *Crisis 2*, the median bank reduced its number of monthly lead originations by 36% relative to *Crisis 1*, and there is a 54% drop in the dollar volume of lead originations relative to *Crisis 1*.

documented view, the financial crisis that originated in the U.S. market damaged exporters more severely. *Crisis 2* and *Crisis 3* results engender a positive and significant coefficient on Ln_MVALUE (at the 5% level), suggesting that large firms are less vulnerable to financial crises. We find no significant coefficient for PBR and past stock returns.

CONCLUSION

Previous studies suggest that, in emerging markets, corporate governance structures affected stock price performance during the East Asian crisis. This chapter is the first report on the relationship between the corporate governance structures and stock price performance during the current financial crisis in an industrialized country (Japan). The analysis is important because some authors argue that the corporate governance structure is a main cause of the U.S. financial institutions' crisis (Adams, 2009). It also contributes to the corporate governance literature by examining whether the recent corporate governance reform helps firms avoid large stock price reductions during a financial crisis.

Our findings are summarized as follows. First, we find evidence that firms that adopt stock option plans suffer more from deteriorating stock price performance. An investment strategy that buys shares of firms not adopting stock options shows 12% lower losses during the entire crisis period than a strategy of investing in firms that use stock options. This result suggests that managerial risk-taking incentives induced by stock option granting make the stock price performance more vulnerable to financial crises. The result is consistent with the finding by Adams (2009) that U.S. banks that received bailout money from TARP have greater incentive pay for CEOs.

Secondly, firms with more non-Japanese shareholders (cross-holding shareholders) experience larger (smaller) stock price reductions. The result sharply contrasts to the evidence presented by Baek (2004) that Korean firms with more unaffiliated foreign shareholders experienced small stock price reductions. For the case of the current financial crisis, it is likely that the exit of foreign investors from the Japanese market had a negative impact on firm value. In contrast, firms with stable shareholders (cross-holding shareholders) are less susceptible to the global economic crisis. Those results suggest that the traditional Japanese corporate ownership structure makes shareholder wealth more stable. Overall, the data suggest that corporate governance structures are important determinants of stock price performance during the financial crisis, even in industrial countries.

Finally, it is apparent that firms that rely on bank financing suffer more from deteriorating stock price performance. This result is consistent with the findings by Kang and Stultz (2000) and Baek et al. (2004). Bank-dependent firms have no alternative financing source. Therefore, it is difficult for them to raise funds during a financial crisis. These companies are also likely to face increased bankruptcy costs when banks face severe conditions.

REFERENCES

Adams, R. (2009). Governance and the financial crisis. Available at SSRN: http://ssrn.com/abstract=1398583.

Baek, J-S., Kang, J-K., & Park, K.S. (2004). Corporate governance and firm value: Evidence from the Korean financial crisis. *Journal of Financial Economics 71*, 265-313.

Bennedsen, M., Kongsted, H.C., & Nielsen, K.M. (2008).The causal effect of board size in the performance of small and medium-sized firms. *Journal of Banking and Finance 32*, 1098-1109.

Boone, A., Field., L, Karpoff, J., & Raheja, C. (2007). The determinants of corporate board size and composition: An empirical analysis. *Journal of Financial Economics 85*, 66-101.

Bordo, M., & Eichengreen, B. (2002). Crisis now and then: what lessons from the last era of financial globalization? NBER Working Paper No. 8716.

Block, J., & Sandner, P. (2009). What is the effect of the financial crisis on venture capital financing? Empirical evidence from US internet start-ups. Available at SSRN: http://ssrn.com/abstract=1373723.

Campello, M., Graham, J.R., & Harvey, C.R. (2009a). The real effects of financial constraints: Evidence from a financial crisis. Available at SSRN: http://ssrn.com/abstract=1318355.

Campello, M., Giambona, E., Graham, J.R., & Harvey, C.R. (2009b). Liquidity management and corporate investment: During a financial crisis. Available at SSRN: http://ssrn.com/abstract=1444009.

Carhart, M. (1997). On persistence in mutual fund performance. *Journal of Finance 52*, 57-82.

Chen, C., Guo, W., & Mande, V. (2003). Managerial ownership and firm valuation: Evidence from Japanese firms. *Pacific-Basin Finance Journal 11*, 267-283.

Coles, J.L., Daniel, N.D., & Naveen, L. (2006). Managerial incentives and risk-taking. *Journal of Financial Economics 79*, 431-468.

Coles, J., Daniel, N., & Naveen, L. (2008). Boards: does one size fit all? *Journal of Financial Economics 87*, 329-356.

Cohen, R., Hall, B., & Viceira, L. (2000). Do executive stock options encourage risk-taking? Working Paper, Harvard Business School.

Datta, S., Iskandar-Datta, M., & Raman, K. (2001). Executive compensation and corporate acquisition decisions. *Journal of Finance 56*, 2299-2336.

DeFusco, R., Johnson, R., & Zorn, T. (1990). The effect of executive stock option plans on stockholders and bondholders. *Journal of Finance 45*, 617–627.

Denis, D., & Sarin, A. (1999). Ownership and board structure in publicly traded corporations, *Journal of Financial Economics 52*, 187-223.

Eisenberg, T., Sundgren, S., & Wells, M. (1998). Larger board size and decreasing firm value in small firms. *Journal of Financial Economics 48*, 35-54.

Fama, E., & French, K.R. (1993). Common risk factors in the returns on stocks and bonds. *Journal of Financial Economics 33*, 3-53.

Fazzari, S., Hubbard R.G., & Petersen, B. (1988). Investment and finance reconsidered. *Brookings Papers on Economic Activities 1*, 141-195.

Guay, W.R. (1999). The sensitivity of CEO wealth to equity risk: An analysis of the magnitude and determinants. *Journal of Financial Economics* 53, 43-71.

Guest, P.M. (2008). The determinants of board size and composition: Evidence from the UK. *Journal of Corporate Finance 14*, 51-72.

Hiraki, T., Inoue, H., Ito, A., Kuroki, F., & Masuda, H. (2003). Corporate governance and firm value in Japan. *Pacific-Basin Finance Journal 11*, 239-265.

Hoshi, T., & Kashyap, A. (2004). Japan's financial crisis and economic stagnation. *Journal of Economic Perspectives 18*, 3–26.

Hoshi, T., Kashyap, A., & Scharfstein, D. (1990). The role of banks in reducing the costs of financial distress in Japan. *Journal of Financial Economics 27*, 67–88.

Hoshi, T., Kashyap, A., & Scharfstein, D. (1991). Corporate structure, liquidity, and investment: Evidence from Japanese industrial groups. *Quarterly Journal of Economics 106*, 33-60.

Ivashina, V., & Scharfstein, D. (2009). Bank lending during the financial crisis of 2008. Available at SSRN: http://ssrn.com/abstract=1297337.

Jensen, M. (1993). The modern industrial revolution, exit, and the failure of internal control system. *Journal of Finance 48*, 831-880.

Johnson, S., Boone, P., Breach, A., & Friedman, E. (2000). Corporate governance in the Asian financial crisis. *Journal of Financial Economics 58*, 141-186.

Kang, J-K., & Stultz, R. (2000). Do banking shocks affect borrowing firm performance? An analysis of the Japanese experience. *Journal of Business 73*, 1-23.

Kato, H.K., Lemmon, M., Luo, M., & Schallheim, J. (2005). An empirical examination of the costs and benefits of executive stock options: Evidence from Japan. *Journal of Financial Economics 78*, 435-461.

La Porta, R., Lopez-de-Silanes, F., Shleifer, A., & Vishny, R.W. (1998). Law and finance. *Journal of Political Economy 106*, 1113-1155.

Lehn, K., Patro, S., & Zhao, M. (2004). *Determinants of the size and structure of corporate boards: 1935–2000.* University of Pittsburgh Working Paper, 2004.

Lemmon, M.L., & Lins, K.V. (2003). Ownership structure, corporate governance, and firm value: Evidence from the East Asian Financial crisis. *Journal of Finance 58*, 1445-1468.

Linck, J.S., Netter, J.F., & Yang, T. (2008). The determinants of board structure. *Journal of Financial Economics 87*, 308-328.

Lipton, M., & Lorsch, J. (1992). A modest proposal for improved corporate governance. *Business Lawyer 48*, 59-77.

Mak, Y, & Li, Y. (2001). Determinants of corporate ownership and board structure: Evidence from Singapore. *Journal of Corporate Finance 7*, 231-256.

McConnell, J., & Servaes, H. (1990). Additional evidence on equity ownership and corporate value. *Journal of Financial Economics 27*, 595–612.

McConnell, J., & Servaes, H. (1995). Equity ownership and the two faces of debt. *Journal of Financial Economics 39*, 131–157.

Mitton, T. (2002). A cross-firm analysis of the impact of corporate governance on the East Asian financial crisis. *Journal of Financial Economics 64*, 215-241.

Miyajima, H., & Kuroki, F. (2007). The unwinding of cross-shareholding in Japan. In M. Aoki, G. Jackson, & H. Miyajima (Eds.). *Corporate Governance in Japan* (pp.79-124). New York: Oxford University Press.

Miyajima, Y., & Nitta, K. (2006). Nihongata torishimariyakukai no tagenteki shinka: sono ketteiyoin to performance koka (Multilateral evolution of Japanese corporate boards: determinants and performance effects), Waseda University Working Paper 06-003 (in Japanese).

Morck, R., & Nakamura, M. (1999). Banks and corporate control in Japan. *Journal of Finance 54*, 319-339.

Morck, R., Nakamura, M., & Shivdasani, A. (2000). Banks, ownership structure, and firm value in Japan. *Journal of Business 73*, 539–567.

Morck, R., Shleifer, A., & Vishney, R. (1988). Management ownership and market valuation. *Journal of Financial Economics 20*, 293–315.

Peek, J., & Rosengren, E. (2005). Unnatural selection: perverse incentives and the misallocation of credit in Japan. *American Economic Review 95*, 1144–1166.

Pinkowitz, L., & Williamson, R. (2001). Bank power and cash holdings: Evidence from Japan. *Review of Financial Studies 14*, 1059–1082.

Sheard, P. (1989). The main bank system and corporate monitoring and control in Japan. *Journal of Economic Behavior and Organization 11*, 399-422.

Uchida, K. (2006). Determinants of stock option use by Japanese companies. *Review of Financial Economics 15*, 251-269.

Uchida, K. (2009a). Do recommendations for small boards increase firms' shareholder value? Evidence from Japan. Available at SSRN: http://ssrn.com/abstract=1460971.

Uchida, K. (2009b). Reduction in bank ownership and firm performance: evidence from Japan. Available at SSRN: http://ssrn.com/abstract=1460344.

Uchida, K., & Matsumoto, M. (2006). Ownership structures and operating performance changes surrounding stock option adoptions: Evidence from Japan. *Corporate Ownership & Control 4*, 10-23.

Weinstein, D.E., & Yafeh, Y. (1998). On the costs of a bank-centered financial system: Evidence from the changing main bank relations in Japan. *Journal of Finance 53*, 635–672.

Whited, T.M. (1992). Debt, liquidity constraints, and corporate investment: Evidence from panel data. *Journal of Finance 47*, 1425-1470.

Yermack, D. (1996). Higher valuations of companies with a small board of directors, *Journal of Financial Economics 40*, 185-212.

In: Financial Crisis in the Global ...
Editors: A. Tomohara, M. Sherlock

ISBN: 978-1-61470-597-0

Chapter 3

U.S. Housing Bubble and Capital Inflows

Andre R. Neveu and Akinori Tomohara

Abstract

In this chapter we discuss the facts surrounding the build-up to the United States housing and financial crisis, paying close attention to the importance of the capital inflows from abroad. In the years leading up to the housing bubble, real estate prices rose very rapidly. The Federal Reserve's use of conventional monetary policy was not effective at raising long-term borrowing rates between 2004 and 2006. This chapter argues that large amounts of foreign purchases occurred during the housing boom, a possible contributing factor to low borrowing costs and rising house prices. The local housing market of Los Angeles is studied to help understand the bubble from a regional perspective.

1. Introduction

The United States housing market began to show signs of "bubble" development during 2005 while Alan Greenspan was chairman of the Federal Reserve's Federal Open Market Committee ("FOMC"). In a now famous statement on the housing market, Chairman Greenspan stated on May 20th, 2005, "Without calling the overall national issue a bubble, it's pretty clear that it's an unsustainable underlying pattern (Greenspan, 2005)". As noted by *The New York Times*, "[Greenspan] acknowledged concerns over "froth" in the market and pointed to a big increase in speculation in homes—particularly in second homes. As a result, he said, there are 'a lot of local bubbles' around the country (Andrews, 2005)." While several proximate causes have been noted for the housing bubbles that occurred across the country, at the time of Greenspan's assessment the U.S. housing market was not overly appreciated in value. However, several markets such as Las Vegas, Los Angeles, Phoenix, and Miami had experienced rampant speculation. Figure 1 shows that housing bubbles were appearing in large cities, but were not yet a nationwide phenomenon.

At the time of Greenspan's statements in May 2005, the 10-city S&P Case-Shiller ("S&P CS") home price index stood at 261.01 (Figure 1). The S&P CS index is a measurement of house prices across the United States, relative to prices at the beginning of the year 2000.[1] By April 2006, the S&P CS 10-city composite index rose another 9.8%, hitting 226.23 as home prices peaked. The peak for the 20-city S&P CS composite index occurred in May 2006. Figure 1 also plots the U.S. Federal Housing Finance Agency ("FHFA") purchase-only price index, which provides information on a more local level. The FHFA price index did not rise as quickly as the S&P CS index, and also did not fall as rapidly.

Figure 1 shows that the FHFA purchase only index declined approximately 10% during 2009, only about half the pace of the S&P CS index. The FHFA provides data on a more localized level than the Case-Shiller index explaining some of the discrepancy between the two indexes. Both the FHFA index and the S&P CS index have shown that on a year-to-year basis, prices are still lower, but on a month-to-month basis, prices began to rise again in mid-2009.

Prices fell 33.1% from the peak in April 2006 through May 2009 when using the S&P CS 10-city composite index. The S&P CS 10-city composite index estimates that home prices had not been at current levels since July 2003. The housing market has shown some improvement in late 2009 as the annual rate of decline in home prices slowed down from the -21% decline seen in December 2008 (Figure 2).[2]

Month-to-month changes in both S&P indexes and the FHFA index all show that home prices increased nationwide in late 2009 (Figure 3). Rising home prices at the monthly level may imply that we have hit the bottom of the market with prices around the same level seen in 2003.

---

[1]The base year was used as January 2000 for the 10- and 20-city composite indexes as well as the FHFA indexes.

[2]Figure 2 is derived using the log difference of the S&P CS 10- and 20-city indexes.

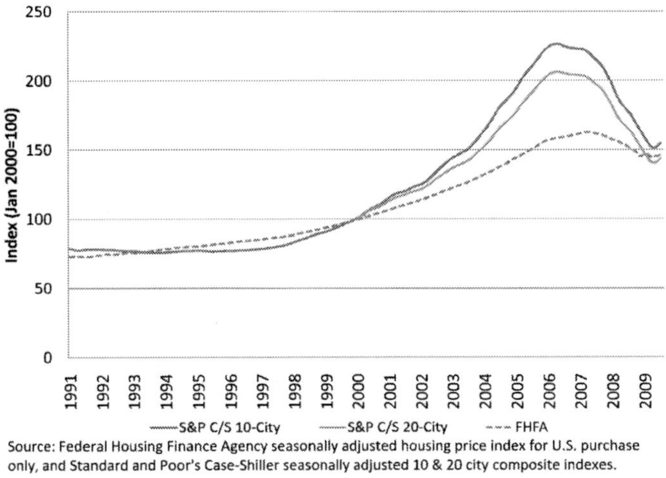

Figure 1. FHFA Total U.S. Purchase Only HPI and S&P Case-Shiller 10-City Composite Index, Seasonally Adjusted (1991=100).

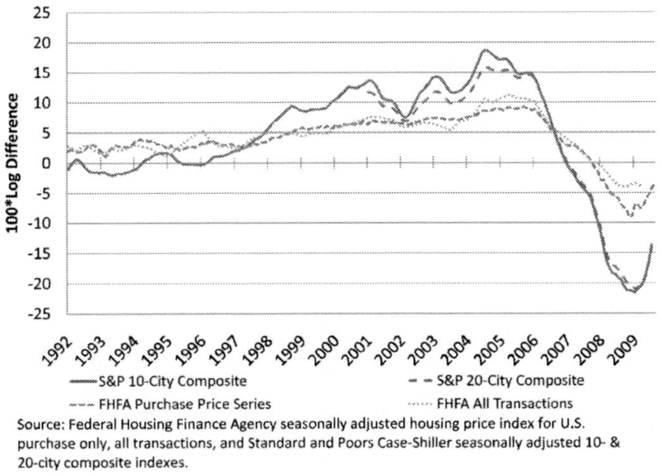

Figure 2. Growth in FHFA and S&P Case-Shiller 10-City Indexes (100*Log Difference) Year-Over-Year Change.

It is difficult to discern the underlying rate of growth in house prices using the S&P or FHFA index data. With the unsustainable rise in home prices over the 2003 to 2006 period, there was also a significant increase in the nationwide supply of homes. The supply increase along with the subsequent price collapse, might lead us to see stagnating home prices in the future rather than returning to some positive trend growth. Figure 4 displays that the 1990's were typified by stagnant or contracting home prices, no doubt related to the Savings and Loan crisis of the late 1980's and early 1990's.

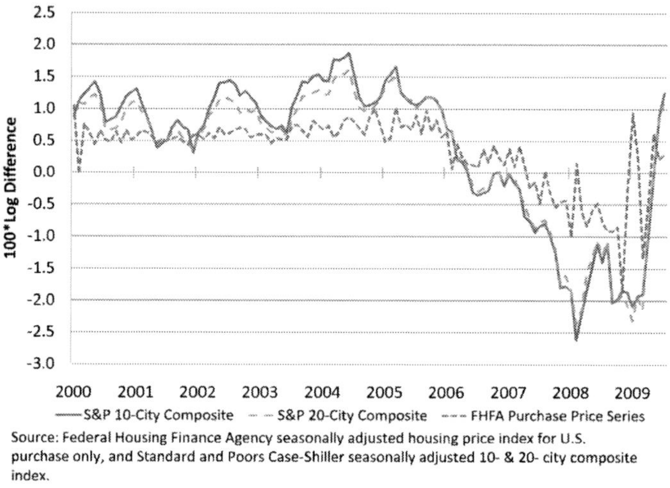

Figure 3. Growth in FHFA Total U.S. Purchase Only and S&P CS 10- and 20-City Composite Indexes (100 Times Log Difference) Month-to-Month Change.

2. Ineffective Monetary Policy

In May 2005, at the time of Greenspan's comments on the froth in local housing markets the Federal Funds rate stood at 3%. By July 2006 the Federal Funds rate had increased to 5.25% (Figure 5). In July 2006, the housing bubble had passed peak price levels in 13 of the 20 cities tracked by the Case-Shiller Index. The housing market peaked only four months after Ben Bernanke was confirmed as successor to Alan Greenspan as chairman of the FOMC.

What is apparent from Figure 5 is that the Fed's control of short-term interest rates did not appear to have much impact on the long-term interest rates that the Fed hopes to control during the 2001–2006 period. While the Fed has the

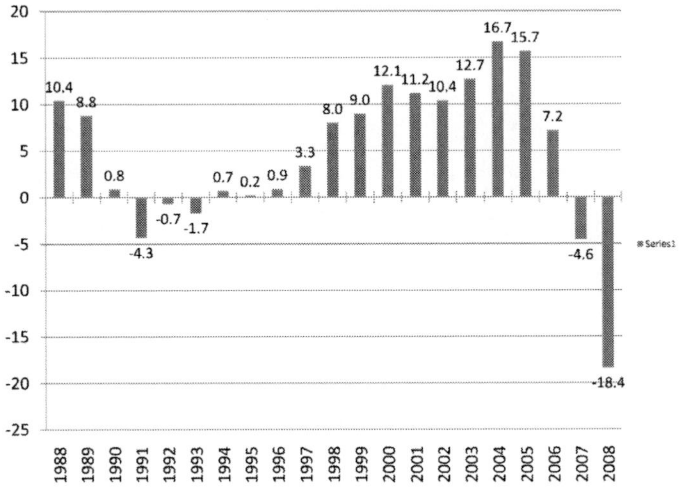

Figure 4. Average Annual Rate of Change S&P CS Index (Average of 100 Times Log Difference).

ability to alter the short-term lending rate, they have less control over longer-term interest rates. Most importantly, longer-term interest rates are more likely to drive most investment and consumption decisions that the Fed was trying to slow by increasing short-term interest rates.

Prior to the 2001 recession, long-term interest rates appeared to be effectively managed by the Federal Reserve through their use of the short-term lending rate. However, the failure of the central bank to raise longer term interest rates following the 2001 recession posed a "conundrum" to Greenspan and other economists. The peculiar behavior of interest rates following the 2001 recession is important to the overall understanding of the buildup of the housing bubble (Backus & Wright, 2007).

Historically, U.S. long-term interest rates moved in tandem with short-term rates (Figure 5). However, long-term interest rates did not respond as expected following increases in Federal Funds rates in the 2004–2007 tightening period.

While Alan Greenspan has been blamed by many for much of the U.S. housing bubble, it was not obvious why traditional contractionary monetary policy did not work when the Fed began to increase short-term rates in 2004. Manipulation of the short-term lending rate through open market operations has been

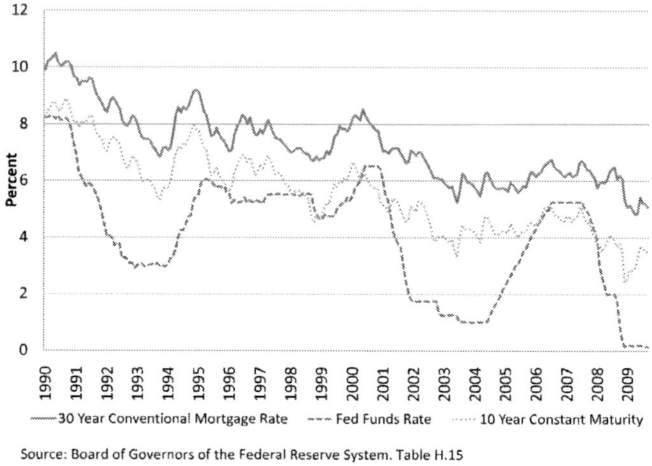

Figure 5. Effective Federal Funds Rate, 30-Year Conventional Mortgage Rate, and 10-Year Constant Maturity Treasury Rate.

the monetary tool of choice used by central bankers who are trying to affect the amount of money and credit available in the economy.

In Figure 2., we can see that the yield curve was very steep on June 29, 2004 just before the Fed began to increase short-term rates. The term spread between 1-month and 20-year Treasury rates on June 29th, 2004, was over 4 percent or 400 basis points. One year later, the Federal Funds rate rose to 3 percent, and the yield curve flattened to a term spread of 138 basis points. By June 29th, 2006, the Federal Funds rate stood at 5.25 percent, and the term spread fell to 71 basis points. Eight months later, in February 2007, the yield curve was inverted, with a negative term spread. Since demand for housing loans relies on the long-term rates, the housing bubble was likely accelerated with relatively low long-term interest rates throughout the entire 2004–2006 tightening period.

The mechanism through which tight monetary policy may have failed to raise long-term rates may partially be due to large capital inflows into the United States. As Figure 7 shows, the level of quarterly capital inflows increased dramatically around 2004. Between 1999 and 2003, annual capital inflows were between 700 billion and 1 trillion dollars. Annual seasonally adjusted capital inflows in 2004, rose to over 1.5 trillion dollars, 79% higher than in 2003. In 2005 total annual capital inflows were over 1.2 trillion, and exceeded 2 trillion

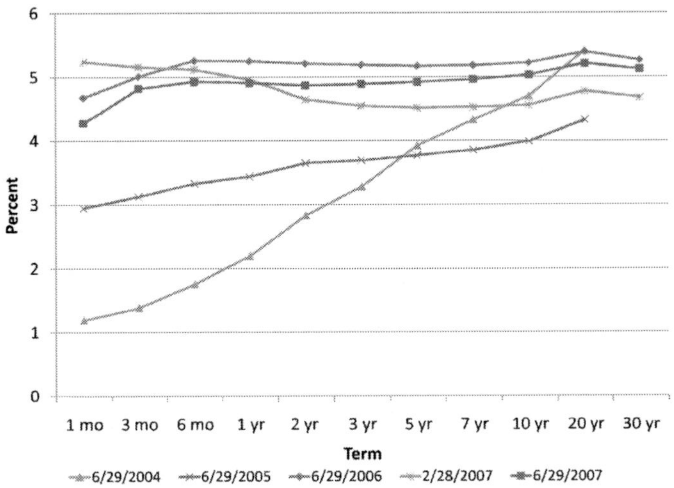

Figure 6. Yield Curve 2004-2007.

in 2006 and 2007. While the Fed can attempt to control the amount of domestic money through interest rate manipulation, capital inflows to long-term assets from foreign countries are not managed by normal Federal Reserve funcitons. The central bank can choose to accommodate capital inflows allowing interest rates to adjust downward thus discouraging more inflows. Alternatively the Fed can attempt to sterilize inflows by selling long-term securities to keep rates high, discouraging further borrowing for consumption or investment. The Fed's standing policy prior to the credit crisis was to manipulate short-term interest rates while passively letting the free market dictate the price of longer-term assets. By passively accommodating foreign capital inflows, long-term rates continued to decline. Meanwhile, mortgage lending continued to escalate while long-term rates remained low between 2005 and 2008.

The literature examines causes of the conundrum and provides various views. While the timing of the rapid increase in capital inflows suggest this as a possible cause of the housing bubble, not all economists are in agreement. Backus & Wright (2007) provided some evidence that the Fed was unable to control long-term interest rates due to a reduced term premium which may have fallen because of lower aggregate volatility, reduced financial market volatility, and more predictable monetary policy. Backus & Wright believe that inflows are at most a minor contributor to the reduction in the term premium. As evidence

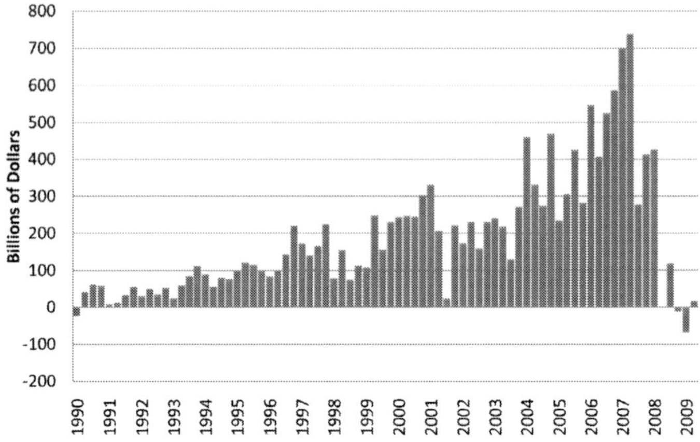

Source: U.S. Bureau of Economic Analysis (Capital inflows are defined as foreign-owned assets in the United States, excluding financial derivatives)

Figure 7. Capital Inflows.

of their position, Backus & Wright show that when China only slightly revalued the renminbi on July 21st, 2005, interest rates for on-the-run 10 year U.S. Treasuries rose by approximately 7 basis points. The signal that the renminbi would be allowed to strengthen against the dollar in the short-term likely would have continued to push rates higher. However, the People's Bank of China continued to accumulate dollars during the next three years under a managed float, albeit at a slower pace than would have occurred under the fixed exchange rate regime. Backus & Wright dismissed foreign inflows as a major cause of the unresponsive long-term interest rates, and believed that inflows were a minor contributor to the reduction in the term premium. The work of Backus & Wright did not directly address house pricing issues however, and does not empirically test their hypothesis beyond the Chinese currency intervention mentioned above.

Evidence provided by Warnock & Warnock (2009) shows that foreign capital inflows have in fact led to changes in mortgage rates and long-term rates in a magnitude that may have been significant enough to drive consumption and home prices higher, supporting the housing bubble of the late 2000s. Increased capital inflows have likely played at least some role in hampering the ability of the Fed to manipulate long-term interest rates. Campbell & Cocco (2007) provide evidence that house prices are related to nationwide borrowing costs, and that increased house prices lead to greater consumption. In similar work, Case et al. (2005) found that there were significant increases in consumption due to increased housing values.

There are some economists who blame former Treasury Secretary Robert Rubin's strong dollar policy for the trend in capital inflows, as the dollar appreciated through 2001 against most major currencies (Figure 8). Following the recession ending in November 2001, the dollar began to depreciate against major currencies, declining approximately 27% in value by the end of 2004. Additionally, in July 2005, the Chinese monetary authorities allowed their currency to strengthen against the U.S. dollar by adjusting to a crawling peg until July 2007 when they returned to a soft peg around 6.83 Yuan per dollar. In the second quarter of 2008 capital inflows slowed dramatically as the global financial crisis took hold.

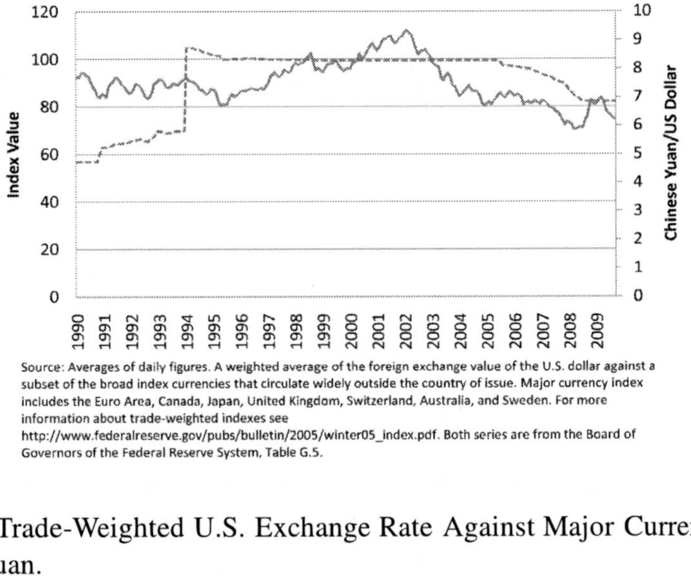

Source: Averages of daily figures. A weighted average of the foreign exchange value of the U.S. dollar against a subset of the broad index currencies that circulate widely outside the country of issue. Major currency index includes the Euro Area, Canada, Japan, United Kingdom, Switzerland, Australia, and Sweden. For more information about trade-weighted indexes see http://www.federalreserve.gov/pubs/bulletin/2005/winter05_index.pdf. Both series are from the Board of Governors of the Federal Reserve System, Table G.5.

Figure 8. Trade-Weighted U.S. Exchange Rate Against Major Currencies and Chinese Yuan.

3. Trade Deficits and Capital Inflows

The large increases in the U.S. trade deficit that occurred during the 1990s and 2000s coincided with an increase in capital inflows from abroad. As seen below in Figure 9, following the improvement of trade relations between the U.S. and China in the early 1990s, the U.S. trade deficit with China began to increase rapidly. The increase of the trade deficit between the U.S. and China can partially be attributed to China's artificially cheap renminbi, but also has likely increased so rapidly because of the increase in the quantity of low-wage manufacturing labor in China. Capital inflows from China and Japan, the two largest individual contributors to the U.S. trade deficit, began topping 50 billion in 2002, and were soon averaging nearly 80 billion quarterly by 2006.[3]

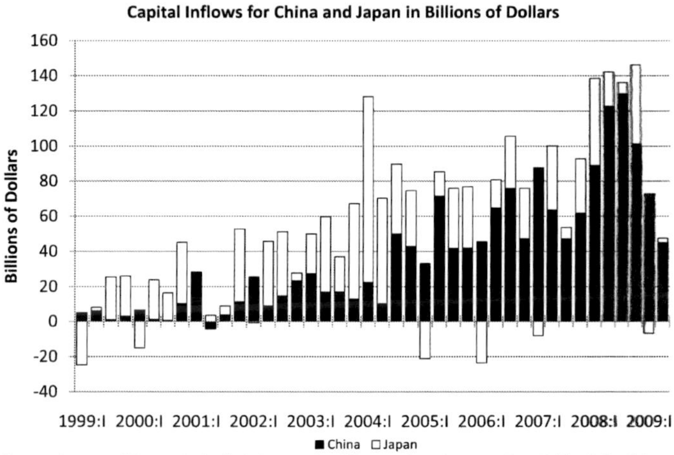

Source: Bureau of Economic Analysis International Transactions Accounts Data Table 12 for China and Japan.

Figure 9. Capital Inflows for China and Japan (Billions of Dollars).

Research by Warnock & Warnock (2009) analyzed Treasury International Capital Reporting System ("TIC") data and provided new evidence that the foreign accumulation of U.S. denominated government and agency debt has significantly lowered U.S. interest rates. As Warnock & Warnock show, by 2005 approximately 51.7% of all marketable U.S. Treasuries were foreign-owned (Warnock & Warnock, 2009).

Our analysis of annual reports by the Treasury Department, Federal Reserve Bank of New York, and the Board of Governors of the Federal Reserve shows that by 2008 the foreign-owned share of all marketable U.S. Treasuries rose to 61.1%, or a total of $2.2 trillion of $3.6 trillion outstanding. In addition to U.S. Treasuries, foreigners increased their holdings of U.S. government agency debt from $0.791 trillion (14.1% of total outstanding) in 2005 to $1.5 trillion (21%

[3]Authors' analysis of Bureau of Economic Analysis ("BEA") data.

of total outstanding) in 2008. In terms of corporate debt, foreigners increased their holdings from $1.7 trillion (19.5% of total outstanding) in 2005 to $2.8 trillion in 2008 (22.6% of total outstanding). Overall, foreign holdings of U.S. debt rose to almost $6.5 trillion in 2008, from $4.1 trillion in 2005, representing 28.1% and 23.5% respectively. In contrast, foreign holdings of U.S. debt were only $0.6 trillion or 10.8% of total debt in 1989, two years before the last trade surplus run by the U.S. in 1991. The average rate of growth in foreign holdings of U.S. debt was 13.6% between 1989 and 2008 using reports produced jointly by the Treasury Department, Federal Reserve Bank of New York, and the Board of Governors of the Federal Reserve ("TFB").

Another interesting finding by Warnock & Warnock was that for additional foreign inflows amounting to 1% of GDP, long-term interest rates would decline by approximately 19 basis points after controlling for inflation expectations, domestic budget deficits, and short-term interest rates. Additional foreign inflows amounting to 1% of GDP were found to significantly depress interest rates on conventional 30-year mortgages by approximately 27 basis points. According to data contained in a 2009 report by TFB and BEA, foreign-owned assets increased in value between 4.5% and 4.9% of nominal GDP between 2004 and 2007.[4] While we cannot directly apply the estimate in Warnock & Warnock without adjusting the underlying assumptions, one can easily imagine capital inflows equivalent of 4% of GDP implying a large reduction in long-term interest rates and mortgage rates.

Backus & Wright (2007) specifically addressed the findings of Warnock & Warnock (2006) which found foreign inflows were responsible for the conundrum. Backus & Wright point out that foreign forward rates in the U.K. and Germany had declined similarly to U.S. forward rates, implying that if U.S. and foreign debt are close substitutes, then Treasury purchases would drive down foreign term premiums. Backus & Wright (2007) and Bernanke et al. (2004) both examine official foreign currency inflows and note that there may be suggestive but inconclusive impacts of these inflows on long-term interest rates. While the conundrum may have been compounded by other domestic and international causes, both Backus & Wright (2007) and Bernanke et al. (2004) admit that foreign inflows likely played some role. Foreign capital inflows accelerated

[4]The increase in stocks of assets held by foreigners is not identical to the flow of new financing, as some assets may have appreciated or depreciated in value from one year to the next. As a first approximation however, these numbers are indicative of the size of international capital inflows to the United States.

after 2005, making it likely interest rates would be further depressed by the increase in accumulation of U.S. assets. Coincidentally, the period after 2005 is when the sub-prime housing market began to accelerate.

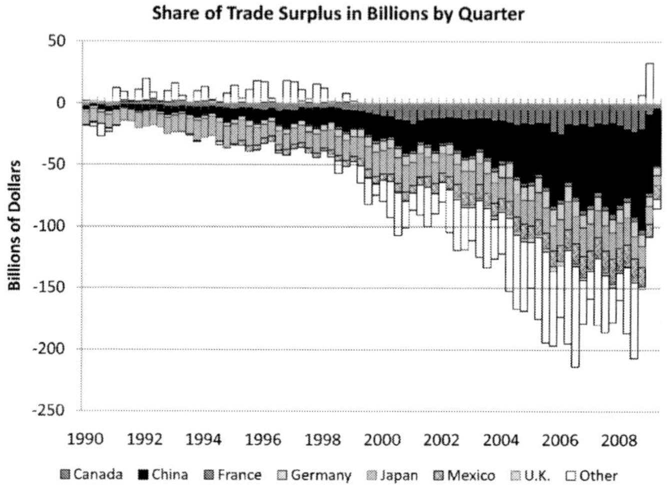

Figure 10. Share of Trade Surplus by Country (Billions of Dollars Per Quarter).

4. Housing Sector

This section considers other factors relevant to our analysis of the housing bubble other than housing prices and capital inflows. The other factors include the spread of non-conventional mortgages, securitization, and the rapid rise in foreclosures and delinquencies. We examine the rise in non-conventional mortgages within Fannie Mae, Freddie Mac, and private mortgage conduits.

4.1. Non-Conventional Mortgages

Table 1 provides evidence that the housing bubble collapse was a broad nationwide occurrence that was felt more severely in some areas. In particular, Las Vegas, NV and Phoenix, AZ saw price declines of over 50% from their peak values. Additionally, all cities tracked by the S&P Case-Shiller 20-city index in

Table 1. Decline From Peak-to-Trough for the 20 Cities in the S&P Case-Shiller Index.

State-City	Percentage Decline From Peak	Peak Month	Trough Month
AZ-Phoenix	-54%	May 06	May 09
CA-Los Angeles	-41%	Apr 06	May 09
CA-San Diego	-42%	Mar 06	May 09
CA-San Francisco	-45%	Feb 06	Apr 09
CO-Denver	-12%	Mar 06	Feb 09
DC-Washington	-33%	Mar 06	Mar 09
FL-Miami	-48%	Dec 06	May 09
FL-Tampa	-41%	May 06	May 09
GA-Atlanta	-22%	Apr 07	May 09
IL-Chicago	-27%	Feb 07	Apr 09
MA-Boston	-18%	Nov 05	Apr 09
MI-Detroit	-45%	Feb 06	Jul 09
MN-Minneapolis	-36%	Apr 06	Apr 09
NC-Charlotte	-11%	Aug 07	Jun 09
NV-Las Vegas	-55%	Apr 06	Jul 09
NY-New York	-21%	May 06	Apr 09
OH-Cleveland	-20%	Jan 06	Mar 09
OR-Portland	-21%	May 07	May 09
TX-Dallas	-9%	Apr 07	Mar 09
WA-Seattle	-22%	May 07	Jul 09
Composite-10	-33%	Apr 06	May 09
Composite-20	-32%	May 06	May 09

California, Florida, and Michigan saw price declines of over 40% from their peak values (Table 1).

The proliferation of easy financing played a major role in the build-up to the peak in the housing market. The terms of non-conventional mortgages played a fundamental role in the build-up and collapse of the housing bubble. The Alt-A mortgage was very popular among borrowers that had less than prime credit or insufficient documentation to secure a conventional mortgage. Mortgage lenders had begun offering several variable rate mortgages through standard adjustable rate mortgages (ARMs) like the popular 2/28. The terms of the 2/28 allowed borrowers to pay a fixed interest rate for two years and a floating rate for 28 years. Another popular mortgage product during the boom was the option ARM. The option ARM gave borrowers the ability to choose their payment, giving them the option of paying less than the entire interest payment or principal each month. If a borrower paid less than their monthly interest payment in an option ARM, the remaining balance is added to the principal. Interest-only mortgages were setup for borrowers who only wanted to repay interest the first two or three years, and then pay principal and interest in the future. The balloon mortgage was also frequently used allowing borrowers to avoid having to repay the entire mortgage over the life of the loan. At the expiration of a balloon mortgage, the borrower would need to make a lump-sum payment of some agreed amount.

There were other mortgage products issued but the aforementioned were the most typical non-conventional mortgages. Borrowers typically chose a non-conventional mortgage when they would not be able to qualify for the fully amortized loan payment. These instruments allowed less qualified borrowers to get larger loans than they otherwise might be able to.

Mortgage lenders employed a practice called risk layering as the sub-prime crisis escalated. A layer of risk might be defined as a borrower who has less down-payment than typically required. A lender might then add a second layer of risk by lending to the same borrower who has insufficient income to pay the fully amortized loan value. The lenders could then add a third layer of risk if the borrower had inadequate documentation of income or assets. Fed Governor Susan Schmidt Bies noted many issues with sub-prime lending standards and risk layering in a January 2007 speech, "Although some lenders may have used elements of nontraditional mortgage products successfully in the past, the recent easing of traditional underwriting controls and the sale of some types of nontraditional products to sub-prime borrowers may generate losses on these products greater than has been observed in the past (Bies, 2007)."

While many commercial banks and loan originators had loosened their lending standards, the presumably safer government sponsored enterprises also had increased their exposure to the sub-prime market through risk layering. Fannie Mae and Freddie Mac held or guaranteed over $5 trillion of the U.S. mortgage market by mid-2008, with billions of Alt-A and ARMs held on their books.[5]

[5]Fannie Mae and Freddie Mac stand for the Federal National Mortgage Association ("FNMA") and the Federal Home Loan Mortgage Corporation ("FHLMC") respectively.

Conforming mortgages purchased by Fannie Mae and Freddie Mac are either held directly by the corporations, or repackaged into securities and resold.[6] Conforming mortgages do not have to necessarily be conventional, but can take the form of the typical 15-year or 30-year conventional fixed-rate loan or one of many adjustable rate mortgage products. As of September 2009, Fannie Mae held over $790 billion in their mortgage portfolio, and had an additional $2,450 billion in pledged mortgage backed securities ("MBS") and guarantees. Freddie Mac held a mortgage portfolio in September 2009 of over $2,240 billion.

Most of the holdings of Fannie Mae and Freddie Mac are conforming conventional mortgages, but they do hold a large amount of non-conventional mortgages for single-family and multi-family homes. Fannie Mae's second quarter 2009 SEC filing showed holdings of nearly $38 billion in adjustable rate mortgages on single family homes, and $22 billion on multi-family homes.[7] Additionally, Fannie Mae held over $58 billion in non-agency structured mortgage securities, over 80% of which was backed by either sub-prime or Alt-A debt. Similarly, Freddie Mac held approximately $109 billion of non-agency mortgage related securities, and another $123 billion in structured agency securities with adjustable interest rates according to their second quarter 2009 SEC filing.[8]

As Figure 11 shows, the largest share of all mortgages are now held by mortgage pools or trusts that include Fannie Mae and Freddie Mac. Over $7.5 trillion in mortgages are held by mortgage pools or trusts, out of the $14.5 trillion dollar U.S. mortgage market. Also included in the $7.5 trillion in mortgage pools are $2.4 trillion in private mortgage conduits. Agency mortgage pools like Fannie Mae hold large amounts of the privately issued mortgage backed securities (Figure 12). Foreign investors have also played a major role in the MBS market holding approximately 21% of agency debt as of June 2008.

4.2. Delinquencies and Foreclosures

On August 20, 2009, the Mortgage Bankers Association ("MBA") issued a press release stating that delinquencies in home mortgages were continuing to increase (Mortgage Bankers Association, 2009).[9] The MBA stated, "...the

[6]Conforming mortgages are defined as those that are less than $417,000 or less in 2009.

[7]See Table 18 of Fannie Mae 10-Q (Morningstar, 2009b), August 6, 2009.

[8]See Table 19 of Freddie Mac 10-Q (Morningstar, 2009a), August 7, 2009.

[9]A mortgage delinquency is defined as those that are at least one payment past due, and do not include foreclosures.

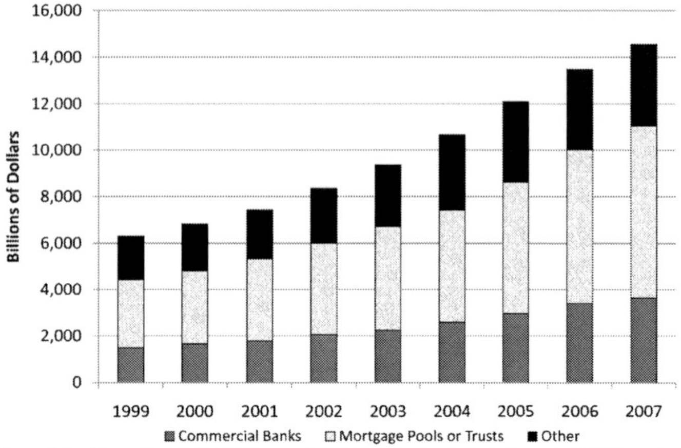

Source: Federal Reserve Bank, Table 1.54 Mortgage Debt Outstanding. Compiled using September 2009 data and discontinued supplemental tables for January in 2004-2008, and December 2008.

Figure 11. Total Mortgages by Major Type of Holder.

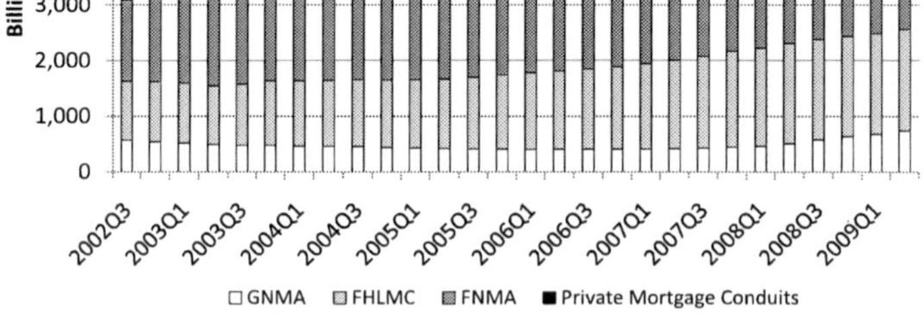

Source: Federal Reserve Bank, Table 1.54 Mortgage Debt Outstanding. Compiled using September 2009 data and discontinued supplemental tables for January in 2004-2008, and December 2008.

Figure 12. Mortgage Pools or Trusts by Type.

percentage of homes in the foreclosure process at the end of the second quarter was 4.30 percent, an increase of 45 basis points from the first quarter of 2009 and 155 basis points from one year ago. The combined percentage of loans in foreclosure and at least one payment past due was 13.16 percent on a non-seasonally adjusted basis, the highest ever recorded in the MBA delinquency survey (Mortgage Bankers Association, 2009)." Foreclosure starts were declining in mid-2009 according to the MBA as 4.13 percent of sub-prime mortgages were entering the process versus 4.65 in the first quarter. However, over 15 percent of sub-prime loans were in the foreclosure process at the midpoint of 2009.

Commercial banks are also tightly intertwined in the mortgage market holding approximately $3,894 billion in mortgage debt in the second quarter of 2009. The commercial banking sector was also reporting increased delinquencies and charge-offs in 2009 (Board of Governors of the Federal Reserve System, 2009). By the second quarter of 2009, delinquencies on loans secured by real estate at commercial banks were over $300 billion dollars (Figure 13). Charge-offs at commercial banks on loans secured by real estate were also rising in 2009 with over $20 billion in write-downs occurring in the second quarter alone (Figure 14).

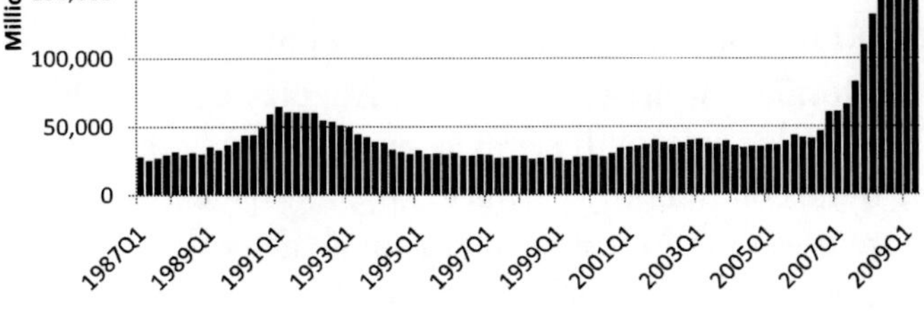

Source: Federal Reserve Bank, Table 1.54 Mortgage Debt Outstanding. Compiled using September 2009 data and discontinued supplemental tables for January in 2004-2008, and December 2008.

Figure 13. Commercial Bank Delinquencies on Assets Backed by Mortgages.

The fact that Fannie Mae and Freddie Mac were taken into receivership in

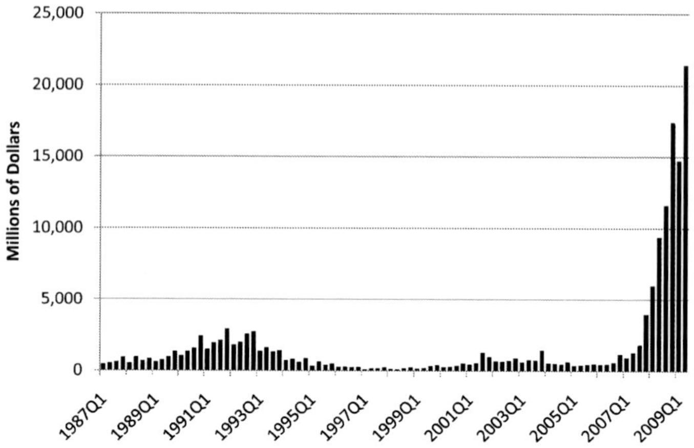

Source: Federal Reserve Bank, Table 1.54 Mortgage Debt Outstanding. Compiled using September 2009 data and discontinued supplemental tables for January in 2004-2008, and December 2008.

Figure 14. Commercial Bank Charge-Offs on Assets Backed by Mortgages.

2008 shows the deep damage to their balance sheets due to the sub-prime mortgage meltdown. Foreclosures and delinquencies have pushed the largest commercial banks in the U.S. to accept Federal bailout money, and the old model of investment banking is now defunct. In the aggregate, rising delinquencies and foreclosures foretell a long path back to solvency for many lending institutions.

5. Los Angeles Case Study

One of the cities hardest hit by the declining housing market was Los Angeles, California. Home prices in Los Angeles declined by an estimated 41% (Table 1). Los Angeles will serve as our case study on housing markets, as we examine trends on building permits and employment in Los Angeles. Building permits are a leading indicator of economic activity, predicting near-term local business conditions.

The building permits data are composed of both residential and non-residential. In Los Angeles the CPI adjusted value of new residential and non-residential permits moved in tandem until 2000 (Figure 15). Following the recession ending in 2001 the path of residential and non-residential building permits began to diverge. The value of residential permits began to increase rapidly, while non-residential permits stayed relatively constant between 2002 and 2007. The increase in the value of residential permits implies the housing bubble was primarily driven by residential housing and not commercial housing investment. Coinciding with the peak in house prices, the value of new residential building permits began to drop dramatically. Additionally, the value of building permits for single family homes fell very rapidly beginning in 2006 (Figure 16). There was also a visible lag between the start of the decline in single and multi-family homes. Renters of apartments provide much more support to the multi-family housing market rather than individual purchasers. The lag between the single and multi-family building permits likely implies that credit (which dried up for single-family home buyers) began to impact the rental-based multi-family housing market in late 2007.

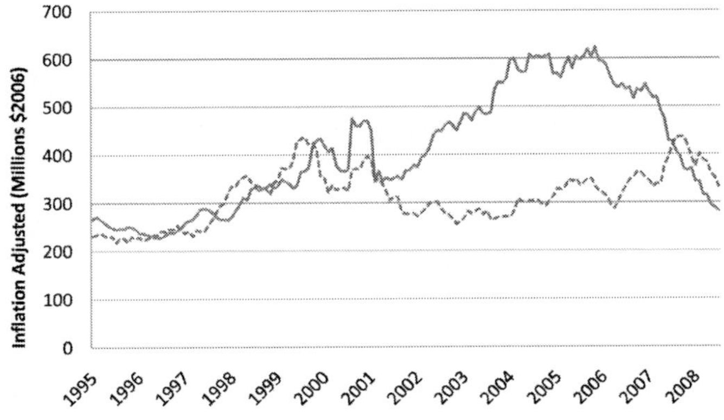

Source: Bureau of the Census for residential and non-residential building permit data, and the Bureau of Labor Statistics Consumer Price Index for Los Angeles. Data show the 6-month moving average.

Figure 15. Building Permits by Valuation, Residential and Non-Residential (Six-Month MA in $2006 Seasonally Adjusted).

Throughout 2008, non-residential and residential building permits were both trending down reflecting a weak economy and pessimistic future expectations. The consumer sentiment index also declined rapidly from July 2007 when it measured over 90, to just above 56 by June 2008. By mid-2009, the housing market appeared to have stabilized.

Leamer (2002) suggests a theoretical model for valuations in the housing market. Under the theory described by Leamer (2002), house prices equate to

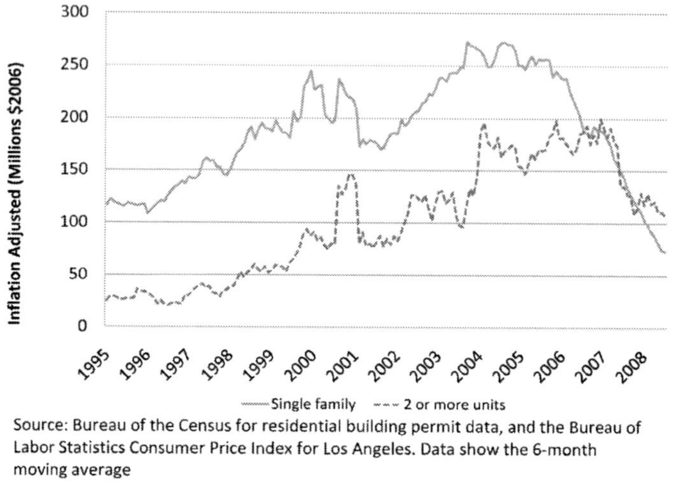

Figure 16. Single and Multi-Family Building Permits by Valuation (Six-Month MA in $2006 Seasonally Adjusted).

the present discounted value of the future rent stream. Following the asset pricing theory for the stock market, we calculate the price-to-earnings ("P/E") ratio for the Los Angeles housing market. Technically, a P/E ratio for homes is calculated as the ratio of the median price of homes divided by the shelter component of the CPI. We estimate the P/E ratio using the shelter CPI as a proxy for annual rental values and the S&P Case-Shiller index as a proxy for house prices. [10] A bubble is created when asset prices deviate from rents stream substantially. The P/E ratios show valuations in the housing market have fallen back into line with the historical trend prior to the collapse of the dot-com bubble.[11]

Los Angeles housing P/E ratios began to increase beyond levels previously seen in 2002 and 2003 when short-term interest rates set by the Federal Reserve were below 2% in an effort to revive the economy after the 2001 recession

[10]Leamer (2002) notes several remarks in utilizing the P/E ratio, "this isn't a perfect measure of earnings, since it is only an index that is arbitrarily set to one in 1996. It is also imperfect because it doesn't net out maintenance and management costs. Most of all, for owner-occupied homes this index is based on the owner's guesstimate of the rental value. Nonetheless, movement over time in this index is going to give us a pretty good idea of movement over time of earnings from homes."

[11]We calculate the level of the P/E ratio between 1987 and 2001 as the historical trend.

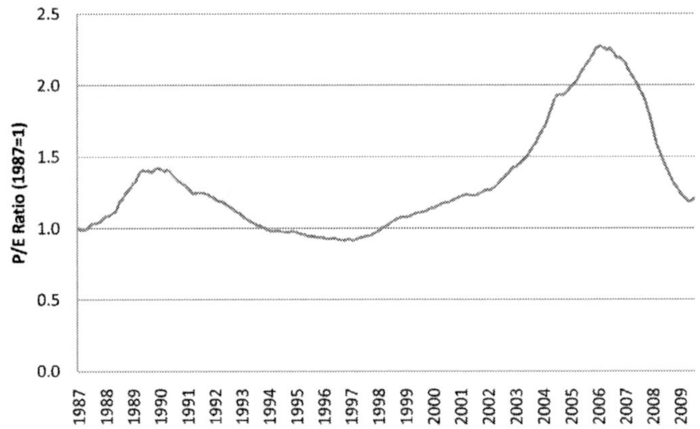

Source: P/E Ratio Calculated as S&P Case-Shiller Index for Los Angeles divided by the Consumer Price Index for shelter in Los Angeles using the base year as 1987.

Figure 17. Price to Earnings Ratio for Housing in Los Angeles (1987=1).

(Figure 17). The P/E ratios rose above 1.5 in mid-2003, which essentially means that house prices were about 50% higher than their corresponding rents relative to their values in 1987. To put this in some perspective, if someone purchased a house for $100,000, using a discount rate of 6%, and using a 30-year life for the house, would imply a monthly rent of about $600 or $7,200 annually yielding a 13.9 for the P/E ratio. If the price of the house rose 100% and the rents did not change, the P/E ratio would double. Similar calculations would hold if, for example rents rose at a much slower rate than house prices.

After hitting the peak in early 2006, the P/E ratio in Los Angeles began to decrease as the housing bubble collapses. By mid-2009 the P/E ratio began to climb again, as house prices ceased falling. The analysis of the P/E ratio in Los Angeles is similar to the nationwide home price index which began to decline in 2006 (Figure 2).

6. Conclusion

The localized housing bubbles that occurred almost simultaneously across the U.S. peaked during 2006. This chapter argues that large foreign capital inflows were at least partially responsible for the housing bubble through the flattening of the yield curve in 2005. When long-term rates did not rise in 2005–

2006, many financial institutions including Fannie Mae and Freddie Mac originated or held an increased number of loans to less credit-worthy borrowers. Increased securitization led to the spreading of foreclosure risk. Fannie Mae and Freddie Mac in particular packaged billions in sub-prime debt and resold it. Fannie Mae and Freddie Mac also managed to hold billions worth of subprime assets individually, as part of securitized investments, or made guarantees on their value. We are now seeing increased charge-offs and delinquencies as large percentage of U.S. homes are underwater, unemployment is rising, and borrowers ability or desire to repay their debts has fallen. Fortunately, as shown in the Los Angeles case study, the price-to-earnings ratios in most cities have come back down to the long-term trend level. Thus, with house prices at or near reasonable levels, it would appear the collapse of the housing bubble is near completion.

One of the primary concerns going forward from 2009, is the Chinese foreign exchange rate policy. The Chinese monetary authorities have called for dollar strength, as the People's Bank of China's investments are at risk if inflation in the U.S. rises to unacceptable levels or the exchange rate weakens. However, in mid-2009, the Chinese monetary authorities maintained a soft peg exchange rate policy with the United States. Without Chinese currency appreciation, the soft peg exchange rate policy and weak Chinese demand for U.S. goods will lead to continued large capital inflows and increased dollar holdings by foreigners. If the soft peg rate policy ends, the U.S. might see a rapid rise in long-term interest rates threatening any recovery that might be underway. In the short-term however, moving to a flexible-exchange rate policy would likely lead to large losses in their own position. The recent capital flow imbalances in the U.S. show that there is a price to be paid if the flows are large and sustained. While the capital flows themselves are not the proximate cause, the large trade imbalances played a major role in allowing for the housing bubble to build. Lax lending standards and securitization helped pile the problems of over-leveraging globally and will likely require several years to recover.

References

Andrews, E. L. (2005). Greenspan Is Concerned About 'Froth' in Housing.

Backus, D. K. & Wright, J. H. (2007). Cracking the Conundrum. Working Paper 13419, National Bureau of Economic Research.

Bernanke, B. S., Reinhart, V. R., & Sack, B. P. (2004). Monetary Policy Alternatives at the Zero Bound: An Empirical Assessment. *Brookings Papers on Economic Activity*, **2**, 1–78.

Bies, S. S. (2007). Remarks by Governor Susan Schmidt Bies at the National Credit Union Administration 2007 Risk Mitigation Summit.

Board of Governors of the Federal Reserve System (2009). Mortgage Debt Outstanding.
http://www.federalreserve.gov/econresdata/releases/mortoutstand/, Table 1.54.

Campbell, J. Y. & Cocco, J. F. (2007). How do House Prices Affect Consumption? Evidence from Micro Data. *Journal of Monetary Economics*, **54**(3), 591 – 621.

Case, K. E., Quigley, J. M., & Shiller, R. J. (2005). Comparing Wealth Effects: The Stock Market versus the Housing Market. *B.E. Journals of Macroeconomics: Advances in Macroeconomics*, **5**(1), 1 – 32.

Greenspan, A. (2005). Remarks by Chairman Alan Greenspan Before the Economic Club of New York.

Leamer, E. E. (2002). Bubble Trouble? You Home Has a P/E Ratio Too. *UCLA Anderson Forecast*.

Morningstar (2009a). Form 10-Q Federal Home Loan Mortgage Corporation-FRE. From http://library.morningstar.com.

Morningstar (2009b). Form 10-Q Federal National Mortgage Association Fannie Mae-FNM. From http://library.morningstar.com.

Mortgage Bankers Association (2009). Delinquencies Continue to Climb, Foreclosures Flat in Latest MBA National Delinquency Survey.

Treasury Department, Federal Reserve Bank of New York, and the Board of Governors of the Federal Reserve (2009). Report on Foreign Holdings of U.S. Securities as of June 30, 2008.

Warnock, F. E. & Warnock, V. C. (2006). International Capital Flows and U.S. Interest Rates. *Manuscript*.

Warnock, F. E. & Warnock, V. C. (2009). International Capital Flows and U.S. Interest Rates. *Journal of International Money and Finance*, **28**(6), 903–919.

In: Financial Crisis in the Global ... ISBN: 978-1-61740-597-0
Editors: A. Tomohara, M. Sherlock

Chapter 4

INTERNATIONAL CONTAGION DURING THE RECENT U.S. FINANCIAL CRISIS

Juan F. Cabrera* and Viktoriya Staneva
Anisfield School of Business, Ramapo College of New Jersey, US

ABSTRACT

This chapter investigates if the shock propagation during the recent U.S. financial crisis can be explained by contagion. It also attempts to determine which pre-crisis macroeconomic conditions make a country more vulnerable to being infected by a crisis. We use heteroskedasticity-adjusted correlation coefficients to test for the contagion from the U.S. stock market to a sample of 27 international stock markets. Comparing the cross-market correlation for the full sample period to the cross-market correlations after the shock we find evidence of contagion in approximately two-thirds of the countries. Furthermore, we find that contagion occurs in countries that have strong pre-crisis macroeconomic similarities to the crisis country. Finally, we perform several robustness tests that leave our main results unaltered.

Keywords: Contagion, U.S. crisis, Transmission channels, Macroeconomic conditions

---

* E-mail address: jcabrera@ramapo.edu. Tel.: (201)684-7354. Corresponding author. An Assistant Professor of Finance at the Anisfield School of Business, Ramapo College of New Jersey.

JEL Classification: F30, F36, F40, G14, G20

I. INTRODUCTION

Despite a disappointing first half in 2002, when the S&P 500 index fell by 196.62 points or approximately 17%,[1] the U.S. market has experienced a period of steady growth and stability from 2002 until 2007. The S&P 500 index experienced a positive return of almost 80% during this period.[2] A major factor behind this economically prosperous period is the steady increase of housing prices during the same 5-year interval. According to the S&P/Case-Schiller U.S. National Home Price Index, home prices generated a positive return of 61% from the 1st quarter of 2002 until the 2nd quarter of 2006.[3] This significant increase in housing prices created a wealth effect, which was at the center of the recent boom in the U.S. economy. More recently, however, this seemingly well-oiled machine abruptly stopped working as the housing bubble burst. The repercussions of the dramatic downturn in the U.S. real estate market have been extremely damaging and far-reaching. During the October, 2007 – March, 2009 period, the S&P 500 index fell approximately 57% to a level of 676.53 points on March 9th, 2009, its lowest level since the late 1990s.

Other countries have experienced a pattern of economic activity similar to that of the United States in the past decade. Table 1 shows the stock market movement for 28 countries (including the United States) during two different periods. As can be clearly seen, during the 2002-2007 period, every country listed experienced a significant gain in the stock market. Poland and Brazil experienced a growth of almost 800%, while India and Russia gained nearly 500% stock market capitalization. During the second period shown, the trend reverses dramatically. From October, 2007 until March, 2009, most stock markets fell by more than 50%. Some markets, such as Russia, Greece, Italy and Poland, declining more than 70%. Overall, this data reveals a strikingly high degree of comovement between a very diverse set of markets (the table also shows the stock market capitalization for each country and the country's region). As we can see, this economic pattern holds for markets of very

---

1 The S&P 500 index value was at 1165.27 on January 2nd, 2002 and it declined to 968.65 points by July 1st, 2002.

2 The exact period referenced here starts on July 22nd, 2002 and ends on July 26th, 2007.

3 The S&P/Case-Schiller U.S. National Home Price Index is a broader composite of single-family home price indices for the nine U.S. Census divisions and is calculated quarterly.

different sizes and for countries exposed to very distinct political and economic risks across the world.

Table 1. Stock Market Capitalization and Index Change

Region	Country	Stock Market Index % Change		Market Capitalization (US$ bill)		
		07/02 to 07/07	10/07 to 03/09	2002	2007	2008
OECD	Australia	239.96%	-65.85%	406.4	1439.8	674.5
	Canada	253.11%	-56.63%	575.3	2346.5	1073.4
	France	159.92%	-60.53%	971.0	2779.6	1499.6
	Germany	193.16%	-58.48%	693.6	2112.4	1114.1
	Greece	233.70%	-74.38%	68.6	264.4	90.6
	Hungary	472.20%	-75.26%	13.1	47.7	18.7
	Italy	136.76%	-71.22%	482.3	1080.8	525.6
	Poland	786.30%	-79.94%	28.7	207.6	90.4
	Spain	244.49%	-59.40%	466.6	1807.6	944.8
	Sweden	248.59%	-65.10%	179.3	611.2	252.0
	Switzerland	133.51%	-51.09%	552.5	1303.7	883.5
	UK	120.66%	-62.08%	1902.3	3897.6	1876.0
	United States	77.93%	-52.31%	11337.5	20420.5	11933.6
East Asia	Hong Kong	129.78%	-56.00%	463.1	1162.6	468.6
	Indonesia	383.33%	-58.53%	30.0	211.8	98.3
	Japan	72.35%	-47.51%	2126.1	4449.6	3221.4
	Malaysia	117.37%	-43.67%	123.9	324.6	212.7
	Taiwan	88.74%	-54.34%	265.6	658.0	370.5
	Thailand	196.20%	-53.68%	46.2	203.9	107.6
	South Korea	275.00%	-68.18%	249.6	1123.6	494.6
Latin America	Argentina	625.53%	-61.75%	99.1	86.0	51.7
	Brazil	797.66%	-52.46%	124.2	1370.6	574.9
	Chile	322.66%	-34.14%	47.6	212.9	132.4
	Mexico	366.38%	-59.75%	111.5	398.7	233.0
Other	China	165.28%	-56.65%	463.1	6226.6	2794.4
	India	511.13%	-63.53%	127.9	1701.8	639.7
	Israel	241.69%	-50.85%	45.9	240.7	136.2
	Russia	480.48%	-72.18%	124.1	1508.0	1378.4

This table shows the percentage change in the stock market index value for two different periods: stable period (07/2002 until 07/2007) and crisis period (10/2007 until 03/2009). It also shows the market capitalization in US$ billions for three different years. The results are presented for all 28 countries sampled. The stock market indices are denominated in USD. Countries are grouped by region.

This chapter attempts to shed light on the linkages between countries in order to explain the strong comovement among such a diverse set of markets. More specifically, it examines whether contagion can partially explain these comovements and explores the factors that may cause a country to be susceptible to financial market contagion.[4] Contagion and the contagious nature of economic and financial crises have been at the center of economic discussion during the last decade. Increased financial integration and the recent popular crises of the 1990s have brought a lot of attention to the issue of cross-country crisis propagation. Prior to the East Asian financial crisis (1997) and the spread to Russia and Latin America in 1998, there was a poor understanding of why country-specific crises could spread internationally. The Asian financial turmoil, which quickly spread to other countries, channeled attention to the issue of international crisis propagation and, more specifically, the contagion phenomenon.

In the past, the literature has addressed the issue of contagion during events of market turmoil that involved mainly emerging countries such as the Tequila crisis (Mexico), Asian crisis (Thailand and others), and the Russian debt crisis. Not only did these crises originate in emerging countries, but most research has focused on the impact of these events on other emerging markets. The financial turbulence during the fall of 1998, when spreads on U.S. corporations rose to almost 200 basis points from a normal level of 100 basis points, suggests that this type of spillover is not limited to emerging markets alone, but can affect a broad spectrum of markets and borrowers. For this reason, we set out to study the global impact of the recent crisis including a wide range of countries. In particular, we attempt to unveil any evidence of excessive spillover from the U.S. stock market to other markets.

A question that crosses most of the literature on financial crisis and contagion is whether the crises are triggered by investors' sentiments and self-validating panic. This question implies that a crisis could spread to other countries simply because of investors' expectations (whether these expectations are rational or irrational). We argue that investors' expectations, which may be unrelated to the economic health of markets, may contribute to the propagation of a crisis. For example, concern over the supply of funds from international lenders of last resort. In the fall of 1998, the IMF had one of the highest usages of its resources, leading to some concern as to whether it would be able to deal with many more liquidity crisis. This could lead the

[4] Contagion will be examined by comparing times of economic turmoil relative to tranquil times. In section III, we offer a more detailed discussion of the definition and channels of contagion.

liquidity crisis in one country to trigger a crisis in another country for fear of any other country being the last eligible for support.

The exact causes of contagion are not known, neither are the precise policy interventions which can effectively reduce it. This suggests the need for a more extensive examination of international financial contagion. Among the many benefits that could be derived from a complete understanding of cross-market shock transmissions, are more effective policy reform and more efficient portfolio formation. First, identifying the channels through which an initial shock is transmitted has serious implications on the effectiveness of short-run isolation policies such as capital controls or temporary rescue packages. If a shock is transmitted mainly through real linkages, the implementation of short-run isolation policies may only temporarily delay the transmission of the crisis, but it will not be sufficient in preventing the necessary long-term market adjustments. If in fact the propagation channels change and are excessive during a crisis, short-run isolation policies could prove very useful in protecting economically sound countries from being infected by the crisis. Second, uncovering significant evidence of contagion would down play the familiar gains from international diversification. Furthermore, it would provide support for certain types of trading strategies, such as contagion strategies.

The remainder of this chapter is as follows. Section II briefly discusses the causes of the recent U.S. financial crisis and proposes a framework of crisis transmission. Section III provides a detailed description of the meaning of contagion, it briefly reviews the literature on the definition of contagion, and offers a unique definition. Section IV discusses the potential channels through which the current crisis could have propagated to other economies. Section V provides an empirical analysis of contagion during the recent U.S. crisis. In this section, we rank countries based on their pre-crisis economic condition, we discuss the data and methodology, and finally, we interpret the empirical results. Section VI performs robustness tests. Section VII briefly concludes.

II. U.S. Crisis and International Contagion

A country-specific shock can begin in either the economy's real sector or in its financial market. It can be safely stated, however, that the recent financial crisis began in the U.S. real sector (specifically, the burst of the housing bubble) and it was propagated to other markets, whether this propagation constituted contagion or not. There are many channels through which a shock can be transmitted to other markets. For example, trade linkages such as trade in goods and services, financial linkages such as the existence of a common creditor or inter-connected creditors (a bank in country A with deposits/loans to a bank in country B), and others. The most plausible channel of shock transmission from the U.S. market to other markets is illustrated in Figure 1.

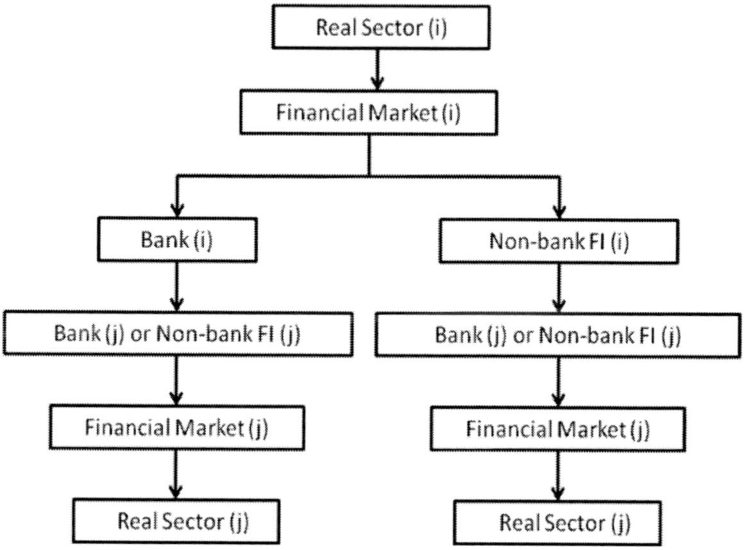

Figure 1. U.S. Crisis Transmission Mechanisms.
This diagram shows two potential transmission mechanisms through which the recent U.S. shock could have propagated to other markets. The United States is referred to as country i and the potentially infected country is labeled by the letter j.

This study does not attempt to analyze the causes of the recent U.S. financial crisis; however, we briefly discuss the issue of shock transmission from the U.S. to other markets. As seen in Figure 1, the origin of the recent crisis can be attributed to the U.S. real sector (i.e. the U.S. housing market).[5] After the heavy decline in U.S. home prices which started in the fall of 2005 and accelerated through 2007, default rate, mostly for subprime loans, began rising. The securitization of these mortgages had placed a large number of these loans in the balance sheet of many financial institutions, mostly non-bank financial institutions such as hedge funds and mutual funds (Non-bank

[5] In Figure 1, the United States would be country i and the other country would be country j.

FI(i) in Figure 1). Financial integration and the existence of heavily interconnected financial institutions across countries spread these real estate contingent assets to most other financial markets (Financial Market(j)), which in turn has had an impact on the real sector of other countries (Real Sector(j)) due to liquidity drying up in their financial markets.[6]

Although Figure 1 shows the possible propagation of the U.S.-originated negative shock through banks as well as non-bank financial institutions, the effect of non-bank financial institutions (hedge funds, mutual funds, proprietary traders, etc.) transmission channels appears to be more significant in the recent financial crisis for several reasons: (1) lack of regulation and supervision of these institutions, (2) relatively larger size of these institutions and their transactions, (3) securitization being mainly a non-bank phenomenon, since banks have restrictions on security investments, (4) liquidity constraints, (5) incentive problems, among others.

Figure 2. Stock Market Indices (USD) – OECD.

This plot shows the time series of the stock market indices of 12 OECD countries and the U.S. stock market index. The time series covers the period from January 1st, 2002 until July 15th, 2009. All indices are denominated in USD. The primary axis (left-hand side) is used to measure the U.S. index, and the secondary axis (right-hand side) is used to measure all other indices. All indices are set equal to 100 on January 1st, 2002.

[6] It is important to mention that the view of the above-described chains as acceptable propagation channels does not imply the existence of contagion in the recent crisis. The existence of contagion would only be justified (according to this study's definition) if the shock were transmitted through one or more behavioral channels.

Figure 3. Stock Market Indices (USD) – Latin America.

This plot shows the time series of the stock market indices of 4 Latin American countries and the U.S. stock market index. The time series covers the period from January 1st, 2002 until July 15th, 2009. All indices are denominated in USD. The primary axis (left-hand side) is used to measure the U.S. index, and the secondary axis (right-hand side) is used to measure all other indices. All indices are set equal to 100 on January 1st, 2002.

Regardless of the exact transmission channels through which the recent crisis has affected other countries, there is overwhelming evidence of its propagation. Figures 2 through 5 show the stock market index of the U.S. against a series of other markets.[7] Figure 2 shows a plot of the U.S. stock market index against a sample of OECD countries. The close comovement among all these countries illustrates an immediately clear pattern. More relevant to this study is the significant decline in these indices following the shock to the U.S. economy. This pattern can be more easily identified in Figure 3. Latin American countries tend to be more closely correlated with the U.S. market, which this figure clearly illustrates. The rest of the figures

[7] Please not that all series are expresses in USD and the proxy used for the U.S. stock market is the S&P 500. Also, all figures show the U.S. index prices on the primary axis (on the left), while the rest of the countries' indices are shown on the secondary axis (on the right).

provide a similar conclusion. The U.S. crisis has had a significant effect on the stock markets and therefore on the economies of a large variety of countries across the globe. This effect, however, could be a consequence of interdependence. The United States, being such a large market, has a significant amount of cross-country linkages. Therefore, a shock to the U.S. is expected to have a significant effect on other countries. The focus of this study is not on interdependence but on contagion. Has contagion been a reason for the spread of the crisis around the globe? To answer that question, we turn our attention to the definition of contagion.

III. DEFINITION OF CONTAGION

There is very little agreement in the economics and financial literature over the appropriate definition of contagion. Although several definitions have been offered, no single definition provides a comprehensive description of cross-market contagion. The most basic definition describes contagion as a shock to one market that is transmitted to another market, but it is not related to fundamentals. This definition captures the essence of contagion; however, it also brings about another level of complexity into the debate: what are these fundamentals? This question does not only represent an obstacle in conceptually understanding the meaning of contagion, but it also creates empirical issues complicating the task of measuring contagion. In other words, a model that attempts to explain and measure cross-market contagion can always be criticized based on the set of fundamentals included.

In order to elude the task of selecting the "true" set of fundamentals, several authors have formulated a broader definition of contagion. They argue that contagion occurs when a shock to one or a group of markets, countries, or institutions, spreads to other markets, or countries, or institutions (Pritsker (2001)). According to this definition, a crisis in one country that spreads to another country due to their strong trade dependence is seen as contagious. We can argue, however, that a shock propagation of this nature is not necessarily contagious but simply the result of interdependence, as it is the consequence of normal bilateral economic activity. This implies that contagion must be defined as a phenomenon that occurs when markets deviate from their normal or stable economic conditions.

Figure 4. Stock Market Indices (USD) - East Asia.

This plot shows the time series of the stock market indices of 7 East Asian countries and the U.S. stock market index. The time series covers the period from January 1st, 2002 until July 15th, 2009. All indices are denominated in USD. The primary axis (left-hand side) is used to measure the U.S. index, and the secondary axis (right-hand side) is used to measure all other indices. All indices are set equal to 100 on January 1st, 2002.

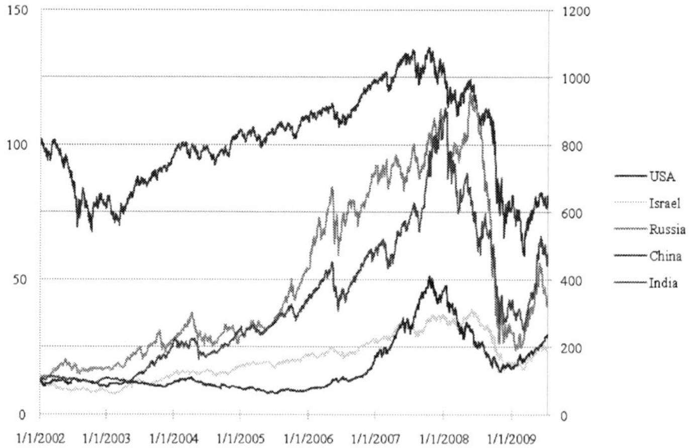

Figure 5. Stock Market Indices (USD) – Other.

This plot shows the time series of the stock market indices of 4 emerging market and the U.S. stock market index. The time series covers the period from January 1st, 2002 until July 15th, 2009. All indices are denominated in USD. The primary axis (left-hand side) is used to measure the U.S. index, and the secondary axis (right-hand side) is used to measure all other indices. All indices are set equal to 100 on January 1st, 2002.

A definition that is widely cited and links contagion to periods of abnormal economic activity defines contagion as an increase in the cross-market linkages during a crisis. This definition has been coined as "shift-contagion" (Forbes and Rigobon (2002)).[8] It highlights that there are many links through which shocks are transmitted in normal times from one country to another, including trade and financial links. The way in which shocks are transmitted, however, does seem to differ during times of crisis. Although, this view of contagion avoids taking a stance on how the shift on cross-market linkages occurs or which transmission channels constitute contagion, it has several important advantages. First, it provides the researcher with a simple framework for testing if contagion exists. As we will see in this chapter, contagion can be measured as a significant increase in the cross-market linkages after a shock. By identifying one period as stable and another as the crisis period, cross-market linkages across periods can be compared. A second advantage is that this definition avoids the selection of the "true" set of fundamentals. In fact the definition does not make any reference to market fundamentals.[9] Finally, this definition does not attempt to find a culprit among the many crisis propagation channels (this is an advantage in the sense that the identification and measurement of these specific channels is very difficult). Instead, this definition can shed light on the type/group of propagation channels that may be to blame for the contagious spread of a crisis.[10] If we find evidence of contagion (an increase in cross-market linkages after a shock), then any transmission channels that are present mainly during a crisis period and not during normal times can be seen as the culprits.

In this study, we propose a unique but related definition of contagion. We define contagion as the transmission of a shock from the crisis market to other markets due to the intensification of behavioral linkages in excess of what is warranted by the pre-crisis economic conditions.[11] Investors' behavior itself, whether rational or irrational, may lead to shocks spilling from one country to

[8] Forbes and Rigobon (2002) termed this definition shift-contagion in order to create a clear distinction between their view of contagion and several other views which may even refer to interdependence.

[9] It is likely, however, that a significant increase in cross-market linkages after a shock may not be related to economic fundamentals, since these fundamentals remain initially unchanged in the non-crisis countries.

[10] Forbes and Rigobon (2002) propose two groups of theories: crisis-contingent theories and non-crisis contingent theories.

[11] The pre-crisis economic conditions include the macroeconomic similarities between the crisis country and non-crisis country, the economic state of the non-crisis country, and the degree of trade and financial interdependence.

another and this spillover may be excessive. There is extensive evidence of the major role of investors' expectations on market movements, especially during periods of heavy market turmoil (i.e. speculative attacks on a currency, banking panics, etc.). This study's definition of contagion argues that investors' behavior intensifies during a crisis making the spread of a crisis to markets that are initially economically sound and relatively independent from the country where the crisis originated possible. Not only do we argue that investors' unwarranted behavior propagates a shock across markets, but we also view investors' psychology as a market fundamental.[12] For this reason, we refrain from using the word "fundamental" in our definition.

It is important to highlight the consistency between our conceptual definition of contagion and shift-contagion as described in Forbes and Rigobon (2002). According to our definition, the significant increase in cross-market linkages is attributed to a change or intensification in the behavior of investors. Therefore, any evidence of an increase in cross-market linkages will indicate the existence of investors' behavior as a contagious transmission channel during a crisis.[13] In order to understand what the intensification in investors' behavior after a shock entails we provide a detailed analysis of the possible transmission channels in the next section.

IV. Transmission Channels: Real versus Behavioral

Generally speaking, there are 3 possibilities of how a shock can "appear" to spread across countries:

- Coincidence – both, countries A and B, get hit with independent country or region specific shocks at the same time. This would not be

[12] Whether the behavior of investors is rational or irrational, it has a very large impact on cross-market linkages. However, in this chapter, we argue that investors need not behave irrationally for the propagation of a crisis to constitute contagion. Rational investors' behavior can produce contagion as long as it leads to the transmission of a shock in excess of what is justified by the pre-crisis economic condition of the affected country.

[13] The consistency of the two definitions will allow us to test for contagion (as defined here) by simply measuring the degree of cross-market comovement before and after the shock.

related to contagion since it does not constitute the spread or transmission of a shock across markets.[14]

- Common shock – both countries are exposed to a common global/regional shock. This would not constitute contagion but it may be seen as interdependence due to geographical and macroeconomic similarities.
- Shock diffusion – a country's or region's specific shock is transmitted to other countries or regions. This *may* constitute contagion if the transmission mechanism is behavioral.

The diffusion of a shock could occur through a variety of channels. This study divides these channels into two main groups: real and behavioral.[15] The distinction between the two groups will shed light on our definition of contagion.

a. Real Transmission Channels

These propagation channels explain how spillovers result from the normal interdependence across markets. Transmission channels during the crisis are not significantly different from those operating before the crisis. These channels are often referred to as real channels because they are based solely on economic conditions.[16]

1) Trade links:
    a. Bilateral exports and imports – a crisis can cause currency depreciation and undermine the competitiveness of its trading partners (creating a bilateral trade deficit). The partner economy will experience a reduction of its exports to the crisis country, and

---

[14] Before testing for the existence of contagion during a crisis, it is important to account for the possibility that two unrelated countries may be experiencing a crisis of their own simultaneously. For example, there is evidence that the co-movements between Asian markets and Latin American markets (such as Colombia) did intensify during the East Asian crisis, even though Colombia has almost no exposure to foreign investors and its trade with Asian countries is insignificant. Colombia will appear to have been infected by the Asian crisis when it could have been a simple coincidence.

[15] Forbes and Rigobon (2002) also divide the many channels into two groups: non-crisis contingent theories and crisis-contingent theories. These classification is analogous to the one presented in their paper.

[16] Calvo and Reinhart (1996) refer to the propagation of a shock through real channels are fundamental-based contagion.

given the bilateral volume of trade, a possible serious reduction in output, GDP growth and employment. Similarly, the exports of the crisis country will increase affecting the domestic sales of the partner country.

b. Third market competition – a real depreciation of the currency of the crisis country may hurt the competitiveness of other countries with similar exporting industries. The exporting industry of the crisis country will be more attractive to other markets relative to its competitors (demand-side effect). There could be, however, an offsetting supply-side effect. The crisis country may experience an output collapse, which will create exporting opportunities for its main competitors.[17]

2) Financial links:
   a. Reduction in trade credit, foreign direct investment and other capital flows – the crisis in one country may limit the ability of that country to engage in FDI, extend credit, etc. Therefore, countries that rely on capital inflows from the crisis country could be negatively affected.
   b. Common creditors – if the crisis country shares a common lender with other countries, a crisis may spread to other economies due to a potential significant reduction in lending from the common creditor.
   c. Interconnected financial institutions – the number and strength of the financial linkages among banks and non-bank financial institutions across countries can be an important factor contributing to the spread of a shock.
   d. Financial instruments – certain types of investment opportunities, such as “emerging market funds”, lump all markets classified as emerging economies together. Therefore, a crisis in one of these emerging economies will spread to other emerging markets as investors withdraw their money from back funds.

[17] This competing hypothesis could be tested. In fact, De Gregorio and Valdes (2000) provide some evidence supporting the latter hypothesis.

3) Market similarities: common macroeconomic conditions may determine asset values in more than one country because of real linkages. Investors "learn" from the initial shock to one country and apply the lessons learned to other countries with similar market structures, policies and macroeconomic conditions.[18]

b. Behavioral Transmission Channels

The transmission of the initial shock could be solely the result of investors' behavior and not of any real linkages across markets. Therefore, these transmission channels cannot be linked to changes in macroeconomic, or any other, pre-crisis conditions.

1) Portfolio strategies – investors may rebalance their portfolio across markets because they follow trading strategies such as momentum strategies, which involve following price trends regardless of beliefs about market fundamentals. Other investors may follow contagion strategies, which would exacerbate the spread of a negative shock across markets.
2) Risk aversion – investors with decreasing relative risk aversion may choose to optimally alter their portfolio holdings towards less risky assets as their wealth declines (or as their risk aversion increases).
3) Cross-market hedging – since international diversification of portfolios involve the cross-market hedging of macroeconomic risks, investors respond to shocks in one country by rebalancing their portfolio through trading in other markets.
4) Competitive devaluation – a crisis in one country will lower the competitiveness of third markets with similar exporting industries, putting pressure on their fixed currencies. Third market governments may devalue their currency to remain competitive. This devaluation could be greater than required by the country's economic position because the third market government may expect a "game" of competitiveness devaluations. Investors may (rationally) react by selling off any assets or curtailing lending in these third markets.
5) Liquidity constraints or endogenous liquidity shocks – a crisis in a country can reduce the liquidity of market participants. If the shock is

[18] If investors' reaction is excessive or unsubstantiated, this propagation would occur through a behavioral channel or contagion

large enough investors may then be forced to sell off securities in other markets to meet margin calls, mutual fund redemptions, or regulatory requirements.

6) Information asymmetries – imperfect information and differences in investors' expectations may lead to herding behavior even when investors are rational. Uninformed investors may decide to follow informed investors and sell off securities in various markets whether the sales are justified by the markets' economic health or not. Uninformed investors may be forced to simply follow informed investors due to the high cost of gathering and processing information, as well as reputational costs. Also, as financial integration intensifies, the number of countries where investments can be placed and the range of investors grows, leading to increased cost of information.[19] In other words, information asymmetries may lead to herd behavior across markets even when investors are rational.
7) Multiple equilibria – changes in investors' expectations that are self-fulfilling in financial markets can cause a country that is economically sound to jump to a bad equilibrium after a shock to another country. For example, during the Asian crisis, two countries with similarly sound economies were affected very differently by the crisis. On one hand, investors responded positively to the depreciation of the Australian dollar during the crisis as Australia's assets appeared undervalued. On the other hand, investors' expectations led to significant capital outflows from Indonesia creating an economic and financial crisis (bad equilibrium) even though Indonesia's 1996 current account deficit was actually smaller than Australia's deficit.

Although, these two groups of transmission channels are very distinct, a simple example can make their differences even more clear. The difference between real and behavioral channels can be illustrated by a scenario where the two countries have common macroeconomic factors. If there is a publicly observable negative shock to country A, and there is perfect public information, this shock will be transmitted through real linkages such as bilateral trade. In a world of imperfect public information, the shock to country A will be privately observable only to some financial market participants in country A (asymmetric information). Therefore, market participants in country B will not be able to discern if the price decline in market A reflects

[19] Refer to Calvo and Mendoza (1998).

information that is relevant to market B, but because of the *possibility* that it is relevant they will cause a decline in market B. This scenario would only constitute contagion if the information revealed in market A is not relevant to market B. Market B would then experience an *excessive* price decline. It is also important to note that this type of contagion need not be considered irrational since investors' behavior is ex-ante rational.

It is also important to highlight that these linkages or transmission channels are not mutually exclusive. For example, asymmetric information coupled with an endogenous liquidity shock could give way to the propagation of a shock, which is contagious in nature. A crisis in country A may trigger massive sales in country B by highly leveraged informed investors, such as hedge funds who need to cover their margin calls (endogenous liquidity shock). Uninformed investors may not recognize that margin calls are the catalyst for the massive sales, believing instead that poor market conditions are motivating these sales (asymmetric information). They may therefore follow the actions of informed investors (herding behavior) causing a severe crisis in country B. A natural question arises, however, regarding the role of investors in spreading a shock across markets: is contagion mainly driven by irrational investors? We address this question next.

c. Is the Behavior of Investors during a Crisis Rational or Irrational?

Irrational contagion can be defined as the transmission of a shock to other countries as a result of investors not maximizing their utility, given their environment and the behavior of other investors in the market. Events such as financial panics (i.e. banking runs), herd behavior, loss of confidence and an increase in risk aversion are frequently used to illustrate irrational behavior. These events, however, need not necessarily reflect irrational behavior. For example, herding behavior could be rational if the investor faces high information costs and reputation costs.[20] Financial panics could be seen as rational if explained by momentum strategies, contagion strategies or self-

[20] Some investors, especially institutional investors, may have a tendency to maintain a reputation that depends on the performance of their portfolio relative to the market portfolio. If the investor faces high reputational costs, he/she may be reluctant to "move" first when new information arrives. Instead, the investor will choose to follow the herd.

validating expectations.[21] Increases in risk aversion may not be irrational if the investor finds it optimal to alter his/her portfolio holdings to less risky assets as their wealth declines (a shock can be seen as a wealth shock to the investor).

In this study, we argue that an increase in cross-market linkages after a shock in excess of what is warranted by the pre-crisis economic conditions of the affected countries does not need to reflect irrational behavior. In fact, we can safely assume the absence of irrational contagion under the assumption that an investor is always making choices that will maximize his/her utility under some constraints. Under this assumption, it is still possible to test for the presence of contagion since rational investors' behavior can trigger an excessive spread of a crisis.

V. Empirical Analysis of Contagion

a. Pre-crisis Economic Conditions

According to our definition, any market reaction in the non-crisis country in excess of what is warranted by the country's pre-crisis economic conditions constitutes contagion. The spread of a shock could then be partially channeled through investors' "excessive" behavior.[22] Therefore, before we perform our empirical test of contagion, we proceed by ranking the sampled countries based on their pre-crisis conditions. The countries are ranked using three criteria: (1) the country's macroeconomic similarity with the U.S. economy, (2) the country's economic condition, and (3) the country's degree of dependence on real links. More specifically, we examine the country's pre-crisis (2002-2006) economic conditions in order to determine if cross-market contagion can be attributed to any one or more of these factors. Once evidence of contagion to a country is found, we can determine the driving factors by looking at the country-specific characteristics before the crisis.

In order to evaluate the pre-crisis economic condition of a country and it's similarities to the conditions in the crisis country, we collect macroeconomic data for each country on the following variables:

---

[21] A contagion strategy consists of selling assets from one country when a crisis hits another country. The selection of assets to sell depends on the cross-market contagion patterns expected by the investor.

[22] "Excessive" behavior in this study refer to behavior that are is in line or do not reflect the true state of the non-crisis country's economy. Any reaction that is misaligned with the true state of the world is considered excessive.

- Fiscal balance/GDP
- Current account/GDP
- GDP annual growth rate
- National Debt/GDP
- CPI inflation rate
- U.S. exports by country (US$ millions)
- U.S. imports by country (US$ millions)
- FDI inward/GDP
- FDI outward/GDP

The data is obtained from several sources, mainly government databases, for the years 2002 through 2006.[23] We consider this 5-year period to be the pre-crisis (stable) period for the purpose of measuring the economic position of each of the 28 countries sampled in this study (including the United States). Using these data, we proceed to construct a single quantitative measure for each of the three criteria listed in the previous section.[24]

The dependence of a given country on real linkages to the U.S. economy (DEP) is measured as the standardized weighted average of the country's total trade volume and total foreign direct investment as a percentage of GDP. The country's economic condition (EC) is measured as the standardized weighted average of the annual GDP growth rate, the fiscal balance, and the inflation rate.[25] Finally, to measure the macroeconomic similarity of a country to the United States (MS), we construct a similarity index analogous to the one developed by De Gregorio and Valdes (2000). [26] All three measures are constructed using a non-linear transformation of the data in order to reduce outliers.

[23] For the national debt data, we were only able to collect data for all 28 countries during the 2 years before the financial crisis (2005 and 2006).

[24] These measures will be calculated for the pre-crisis years (2002-2006) and then they will be averaged out (weighted average with higher weights for years closer to the crisis year, 2007) to get a single statistic of the pre-crisis macroeconomic conditions.

[25] The weights (w_i) are used to penalize a higher inflation rate, a higher fiscal balance and a lower growth rate.

[26] We standardized the variables by subtracting the cross-country average from it and dividing it by the cross-country standard deviation.

$$MS_j = \frac{100}{MAX_{Value}} \cdot e^{-\left\{\sum_i^{nMS} \left[\left(\sum_k w_k \left|x_{j,k,i} - x_{US,k,i}\right|\right)\right]\right\}} \quad (1)$$

$$EC_j = \frac{100}{MAX_{Value}} \cdot e^{\left\{\frac{\sum_i^{nEC} w_i \left(\sum_k w_k x_{j,k,i}\right)}{n_{EC}}\right\}} \quad (2)$$

$$DEP_j = \frac{100}{MAX_{Value}} \cdot e^{\left\{\frac{\sum_i^{nDEP} \sum_k w_k x_{j,k,i}}{n_{DEP}}\right\}} \quad (3)$$

where $x_{j,k,i}$ is the standardized variable i for country j in year k, w_k is the weight for year k, and w_i is the weight for variable i.[27] The weights for the years 2002 through 2006 are 0.1, 0.15, 0.2, 0.25, and 0.3, respectively.[28] n_{EC} is the number of variables used to construct the economic condition measure, n_{DEP} is the number of variables used to construct the dependence measure, and n_{MS} is the number of variables used to construct the macroeconomic similarity index. All measures are expressed as a percentage of the cross-country maximum. The construction of the macroeconomic similarity index includes the annual GDP growth rate, current account balance, inflation rate, national debt, and fiscal balance.

Table 2 presents the quantitative results for each of the three criteria across all 27 countries (excluding the Unites States). The table ranks the countries based on these criteria. Countries with a Q1 ranking are in the top 25% of the sample for that given category. Countries with a Q4 ranking are in the bottom 25%. For example, Canada has a similar macroeconomic structure to that of the U.S. (its MS ranking is Q1), it is highly dependent on trade and financial links (DEP ranking is Q1), and it is relatively economically sound (EC ranking is Q2).

---

27 w_i is equal to +1 for the GDP growth rate and fiscal balance variables, and -1 for the inflation rate variable.

28 For the national debt variable, we only have two full years of data. Therefore, the weights are 0.4 and 0.6 for 2005 and 2006, respectively. For the FDI variable, we only have 4 full years of data (South Korea does not have data available for 2002). The weights for FDI are 0.1, 0.2, 0.3, and 0.4 for the years 2003, 2004, 2005, and 2006, respectively. All weights are selected on an ad hoc basis to give more importance to the years near the eruption of the crisis.

Table 2. Pre-Crisis Economic Conditions – Rankings

Region	Country	Pre-Crisis Economic Conditions		
		MS(j)	EC(j)	DEP(j)
OECD	Australia	Q4	Q2	Q3
	Canada	Q1	Q2	Q1
	France	Q4	Q4	Q2
	Germany	Q4	Q4	Q2
	Greece	Q2	Q4	Q4
	Hungary	Q2	Q4	Q3
	Italy	Q4	Q4	Q3
	Poland	Q1	Q3	Q4
	Spain	Q2	Q2	Q3
	Sweden	Q3	Q1	Q2
	Switzerland	Q3	Q2	Q1
	UK	Q2	Q3	Q2
East Asia	Hong Kong	Q3	Q1	Q1
	Indonesia	Q3	Q4	Q4
	Japan	Q4	Q3	Q1
	Malaysia	Q4	Q3	Q2
	Taiwan	Q1	Q1	Q2
	Thailand	Q4	Q2	Q4
	South Korea	Q2	Q1	Q3
Latin America	Argentina	Q3	Q3	Q4
	Brazil	Q3	Q4	Q3
	Chile	Q1	Q1	Q2
	Mexico	Q2	Q3	Q1
Other	China	Q3	Q1	Q1
	India	Q1	Q2	Q4
	Israel	Q2	Q3	Q3
	Russia	Q1	Q2	Q4

This table ranks all 27 countries (excluding the U.S.) based on three pre-crisis macroeconomic criteria: the country's macroeconomic similarity with the U.S. economy (MS_j), the country's economic condition (EC_j), and the country's degree of dependence on real links (DEP_j). Q1 indicates that the country is ranked in the top 25% of all countries listed and Q4 indicates that the country is ranked in the bottom 25% of all countries listed. Countries are grouped by region.

Among the countries with highly similar pre-crisis macroeconomic characteristics to that of the U.S. are Canada, Taiwan, India and Russia. Surprisingly, 5 out of the 6 countries in the top 25%, when measured by the pre-crisis economic condition criterion, are located outside the OECD group, with most of them located in East Asia. As expected, Canada and Mexico are two of the countries in the top 25% of the countries when measured by the external dependence criterion (dependence on trade and financial links). Several OECD countries (France, Germany, Italy, Sweden and Switzerland) and several East Asian countries (Japan, Malaysia and Thailand) have macroeconomic conditions in severe contrast with that of the United States. Contrasting these findings to our evidence of contagion across our sample countries will help us determine which pre-crisis country-specific characteristics are associated with a higher probability of contagion.

b. Data and Methodology

In order to test for contagion during the recent financial crisis, we use a widely popular statistic: bilateral correlation coefficients. This statistic measures the correlation in returns between two markets. Using sub-samples, we compare the correlation coefficient between two markets during the stable period before the shock to the correlation coefficient during the full sample period. A significant increase of the correlation coefficient would suggest that the transmission channels between the markets have either changed or intensified after the shock. Such a result would constitute contagion.

The empirical literature has implemented several different methodologies to test for the existence of contagion across markets during several well-known crises (Tequila crisis, Asian crisis, Russian default, etc.). For example, some methodologies involve the use of ARCH-type frameworks, while others rely on cointegration between market prices. Contagion, however, has traditionally been measured using bilateral correlation coefficients. Not only is this measure the most popular technique in the literature, but also and more importantly, it is straightforward to implement and interpret.

Although, bilateral correlation coefficients provide a simple test for contagion, Forbes and Rigobon (2002) have shown that changes in market volatility can create an upward bias in the estimated coefficients. Correlation coefficients are conditional on changes in the volatility of the markets.[29] Since

[29] Unadjusted correlation coefficients are conditional on the volatility of the market (heteroskedasticity in market returns). This means that an increase in market volatility can

markets tend to be more volatile during a crisis period, conditional correlation coefficients will tend to increase after the crisis, even if the unconditional correlation coefficient is the same during the stable period.[30] Therefore, calculations based on the unadjusted correlation coefficients may show a significant increase in the bilateral correlation coefficient simply because of the increase in market volatility after the shock, and not because the cross-market linkages have changed or intensified.

To correct for the upward bias due to an increase in the variation of returns after the shock, Forbes and Rigobon (2002) developed a bias-adjusted bilateral correlation coefficient (henceforth, adjusted correlation coefficient).[31] They show the construction of the adjusted correlation coefficient in a two-market model with no omitted variables or endogeneity between markets. Assume that x_t and y_t are stochastic variables which represent stock market returns in two different markets:

$$y_t = \alpha + \beta x_t + \epsilon_t \tag{4}$$

where:

$$E[\epsilon_t] = 0 \tag{5}$$

$$E[\epsilon_t^2] = \sigma^2 < \infty \tag{6}$$

$$E[x_t \, \epsilon_t] = 0 \tag{7}$$

In this model, x_t is assumed to be the crisis country and y_t is the country potentially vulnerable to the spread of the shock.[32] If we divide the sample into two groups, so that the variance of x_t is lower in one group (L) and higher in the second group (H), then the low-variance group is the period of stability before the shock, and the high-variance sub-sample is the crisis period (directly after the shock). The model implies that β is the true relationship between markets or a measure of the degree of cross-market comovement. Also, by construction:

affect the estimates of cross-market unadjusted correlation coefficients even when the underlying cross-market linkages (transmission channels) remain constant or unchanged.

30 Unconditional correlation coefficients have been adjusted for the upward bias created by the increase in market volatility after the shock. We will refer to this type of correlation coefficient as the adjusted correlation coefficient.

31 It can also be termed heteroskedasticity-adjusted correlation coefficient.

32 Also, note that the model does not make any further assumptions about the distribution of the residuals.

$$\sigma_{xx}^{H} > \sigma_{xx}^{L} \tag{8}$$

Using this model, Forbes and Rigobon (2002) show that the adjusted correlation coefficient (ρ_A) can be written as a function of the unadjusted correlation coefficient (ρ_U):

$$\rho_A = \frac{\rho_U}{\sqrt{1 + \theta[1 - \rho_U^2]}} \tag{9}$$

where θ is the relative increase in the variance of x_t :

$$\theta \equiv \frac{\sigma_{xx}^{H}}{\sigma_{xx}^{L}} - 1 \tag{10}$$

Implicit in this set of equations is the relationship between the unadjusted correlation coefficient and the relative variance of x_t. With some simple manipulation, it can be shown that ρ_U is an increasing function of θ given some value of ρ_A.[33] Therefore, during periods of high market volatility, the estimated unadjusted correlation coefficient will be greater than the adjusted correlation coefficient even though the cross-market linkages have not changed.

As mentioned above, this simple model makes two restrictive assumptions. It assumes that there are no omitted variables or endogeneity between the two markets.[34] Intuitively, these assumptions imply that this hypothetical world does not experience any exogenous global shocks and there is no feedback from country y to country x. However, Forbes and Rigobon (2002) show that equation (9) is a good approximation of the adjusted correlation coefficient if the change in the variance of returns in the crisis country is greater in the crisis period than in the stable one (market volatility must increase significantly), and if it is possible to identify the country where

[33] Please refer to Forbes and Rigobon (2002) for a more detailed explanation and the proof of the above-presented equations.

[34] Although the model adjusts for the presence of heteroskedasticity in the stock market returns of the crisis country, it does not adjust for potential endogeneity or the presence of omitted variables. Forbes and Rigobon (2002) show that it is not possible to predict the extent of the bias in the estimates of the unadjusted correlation coefficient when heteroskedasticity is combined with either of these problems.

the crisis originates. In this study, the source or country where the crisis originated is clear: the U.S. market. Furthermore, our data suggests that the variance of returns in the U.S. market (crisis country) increased significantly after the shock.[35]

Following Forbes and Rigobon (2002), we utilize a bivariate VAR framework to estimate the unadjusted correlation coefficient. The VAR framework will allow us to control for serial correlation in stock market returns, exogenous global shocks, and monetary policy coordination.

$$X_t = \Phi(L)X_t + \Psi(L)I_t^{US} + v_t \tag{11}$$

$$X_t \equiv \{x_t^{US}, x_t^j\}' \tag{12}$$

where x_t^{US} is the stock market return on the crisis country; x_t^j is the stock market return in another market j; X_t is the transposed vector of stock returns; $\Phi(L)$ and $\Psi(L)$ are vectors of lags; I_t^{US} is the short-term interest rate for the United States. Finally, v_t is a vector of reduced-form errors. Using the estimated variance-covariance matrices for each pair of countries, we obtain the unadjusted correlation coefficients for the stable, crisis and full periods. The stock market returns are calculated from index values as rolling average two-day returns. The average two-day returns will allow us to control for different market operating hours in different countries. The main empirical framework consists of two-day U.S. dollar stock market returns within a five-lag VAR for each set of variables, X_t and I_t^{US}, in order to control for serial correlation and any within-week variation in trading patterns.

The data was obtained from DataStream and it consists of daily index prices for 28 different countries (including the United States) with very distinct characteristics. We obtained index prices in U.S. dollars and in the local currency. The full sample period covered in this study starts on the first business day of 2002 and it ends on July 15th, 2009. We selected the period 2002-2006 (and a portion of 2007 and/or 2008 depending on the ad hoc crisis

[35] Note that we test for contagion using an ad hoc identification of the periods of high and low volatility (crisis "point") based on relevant news events. It is also possible to test for structural break in the volatility series to identify significant changes in the volatility of returns. The latter method of identification, however, would not be economically meaningful and it would not be practical for policy purposes. For this reason, we choose to test for contagion using not one but two crisis "points" selected on an ad hoc basis. The selection of several turning points could also be seen as a robustness test for the results presented in this chapter.

"point" used) to be the stable period. These years reflect a period of relative tranquility in the U.S. economy. The period after the crisis "point" until July, 2009 will be used as the crisis period.

In this study, we chose two financial events as the crisis "points." The first event, that will identify the break in the volatility series for our sample, is the day when Lehman Brothers filed for Chapter 11 bankruptcy protection (September 15th, 2008). This is the largest bankruptcy filing in the history of the United States and potentially a trigger event for the crisis. At that point in time, however, there was widespread evidence that the U.S. financial system was in trouble. Therefore, to account for the forward-looking behavior of investors, we select the a second crisis point - the day Bear Stearns & Co. informed investors in two of its funds, the High-Grade Structured Credit Strategies Enhanced Leverage Fund and the High-Grade Structured Credit Fund that it was halting redemptions. This event occurred earlier in the U.S. crisis timeline (June 7th, 2007). In summary, all contagion tests will be performed using two crisis-triggering events.

c. Empirical Results

As we mentioned earlier, our coefficient estimates can provide a good approximation of the adjusted correlation across markets if the variance of the U.S. stock market returns increases significantly after the shock. Table 3 and Table 4 present the summary statistics of the stock market returns for all countries in the sample. It shows the minimum, maximum and standard deviation of returns during the stable period, the crisis period and the entire sample period. Table 3 shows the summary statistics when the periods are divided using September 15th, 2008 as the shock date. The standard deviation of U.S. returns more than doubles when comparing the crisis period to the pre-crisis (stable) period. If we use June 7th, 2007 as the triggering event as shown in Table 4, the standard deviation of returns shows similar results. The selection of these two dates should provide a good approximation of any potential increase in cross-market linkages. It is also worth mentioning that the standard deviation of returns for *all* countries increases significantly after the shock, regardless of which date we use as the triggering event. In some cases, the volatility of returns increases by a factor of 3 (i.e. Canada, Hungary, U.K., and Russia).

This chapter's main results are shown in Table 5 and Table 6. All tests on these tables are performed using stock market returns obtained from indices denominated in USD. Also, market returns are calculated as 2-day rolling average returns. Furthermore, both tables present correlation coefficients obtained from the variance-covariance matrix extracted from a VAR framework with 5 lags for all variables.

Table 5 shows the test for contagion based on the belief that the bankruptcy of Lehman Brothers was a turning point in the U.S. crisis timeline. Therefore, we define the stable period as January 1st, 2002, to the start of the crisis period on September 15th, 2008. Using a VAR model, we estimate the unadjusted correlation coefficients, r_U, for the stable, crisis and full periods. Using the bias adjustment in equation (9), we estimate the heteroskedasticity-adjusted correlation coefficient, r_A. Then we use the adjusted correlation coefficients to perform our tests for contagion. More specifically, we use t-tests to evaluate if there is a significant increase in the crisis-period correlation coefficient relative to the full-period correlation coefficient.[36] If ρ_A^F is the adjusted correlation coefficient for the full period, and ρ_A^C is the correlation coefficient for the crisis period, the test hypotheses are,

$$\begin{aligned} H_0 &= \rho_A^F \geq \rho_A^C \\ H_1 &= \rho_A^F < \rho_A^C \end{aligned} \tag{13}$$

The critical value at the 5% level of significance is 1.645. Therefore, any test statistic greater than the critical value will indicate evidence of contagion to that specific country. A "Y" indicator under the "Contagion?" column indicates that the country has been a victim of financial contagion from the crisis originated in the United States. Table 5 also shows the unadjusted correlation coefficients and a contagion test for each country based on these coefficients. In this discussion, we will focus on the adjusted correlation results due to its superiority, as it controls for changing market volatility.

36 We could also compare the crisis correlation coefficient to the pre-crisis correlation coefficient. However, a test of contagion using the full-period correlation coefficient is a more conservative approach and would provide stronger results as the full period combined the correlations before and after the shock. Furthermore, we use the full period as the benchmark in order to be consistent with the existing literature.

Table 3. Summary Statistics of Stock Market Returns (Lehman Brothers Crisis Point)

Region	Country	Pre-Crisis Period 01/01/2002 - 09/15/2008 N = 1747			Crisis Period 09/16/2008 - 07/15/2009 N = 217			Full Period 01/01/2002 - 07/15/2009 N = 1964		
		Min	Max	Std	Min	Max	Std	Min	Max	Std
OECD	United States	-0.070	0.063	0.012	-0.094	0.093	0.029	-0.093	0.101	0.016
	Australia	-0.092	0.090	0.015	-0.152	0.114	0.044	-0.152	0.114	0.020
	Canada	-0.077	0.045	0.014	-0.137	0.150	0.044	-0.137	0.150	0.020
	France	-0.106	0.096	0.016	-0.096	0.128	0.039	-0.106	0.128	0.020
	Germany	-0.115	0.084	0.018	-0.097	0.119	0.040	-0.115	0.119	0.021
	Greece	-0.071	0.077	0.016	-0.153	0.132	0.042	-0.153	0.132	0.020
	Hungary	-0.085	0.078	0.020	-0.211	0.245	0.060	-0.211	0.245	0.027
	Italy	-0.082	0.050	0.014	-0.110	0.120	0.043	-0.110	0.120	0.019
	Poland	-0.076	0.070	0.017	-0.149	0.135	0.044	-0.149	0.135	0.022
	Spain	-0.078	0.057	0.014	-0.127	0.124	0.040	-0.127	0.124	0.019
	Sweden	-0.110	0.083	0.018	-0.111	0.132	0.048	-0.111	0.132	0.023
	Switzerland	-0.100	0.075	0.014	-0.107	0.087	0.030	-0.107	0.087	0.017
	UK	-0.082	0.061	0.013	-0.105	0.140	0.040	-0.105	0.140	0.018
East Asia	Hong Kong	-0.101	0.065	0.015	-0.172	0.136	0.040	-0.172	0.136	0.020
	Indonesia	-0.152	0.082	0.021	-0.201	0.150	0.044	-0.201	0.150	0.025
	Japan	-0.089	0.063	0.016	-0.083	0.113	0.028	-0.089	0.113	0.017
	Malaysia	-0.098	0.046	0.011	-0.056	0.054	0.019	-0.098	0.054	0.013
	Taiwan	-0.086	0.084	0.019	-0.083	0.097	0.033	-0.086	0.097	0.021
	Thailand	-0.128	0.064	0.018	-0.148	0.104	0.033	-0.148	0.104	0.021
	South Korea	-0.105	0.105	0.026	-0.212	0.209	0.055	-0.212	0.209	0.031
Latin America	Argentina	-0.333	0.234	0.029	-0.188	0.108	0.045	-0.333	0.234	0.031
	Brazil	-0.124	0.129	0.029	-0.210	0.184	0.059	-0.210	0.184	0.034
	Chile	-0.053	0.053	0.013	-0.118	0.106	0.031	-0.118	0.106	0.016
	Mexico	-0.072	0.083	0.018	-0.169	0.137	0.048	-0.169	0.137	0.023
Other	China	-0.088	0.104	0.020	-0.062	0.120	0.028	-0.088	0.120	0.021

This table presents the summary statistics (minimum, maximum and standard deviation) of two-day stock market returns for the full sample period, the pre-crisis period and the crisis period. We use the Lehman Brothers bankruptcy filing date as the crisis “point” (September 15th, 2008) in order to divide the full sample into the two sub-samples: pre-crisis period and crisis period. Countries are grouped by region.

Table 4. Summary Statistics of Stock Market Returns (Bear Stearns & Co. Crisis Point)

		Pre-Crisis Period 01/01/2002 - 06/07/2007 N = 1415			Crisis Period 06/08/2007 - 07/15/2009 N = 549			Full Period 01/01/2002 - 07/15/2009 N = 1964		
Region	**Country**	**Min**	**Max**	**Std**	**Min**	**Max**	**Std**	**Min**	**Max**	**Std**
OECD	United States	-0.0695	0.0632	0.0115	-0.0930	0.1010	0.0228	-0.0930	0.1010	0.0155
	Australia	-0.0503	0.0402	0.0119	-0.1519	0.1136	0.0331	-0.1519	0.1136	0.0203
	Canada	-0.0771	0.0455	0.0124	-0.1373	0.1503	0.0314	-0.1373	0.1503	0.0197
	France	-0.1063	0.0963	0.0158	-0.0961	0.1275	0.0282	-0.1063	0.1275	0.0201
	Germany	-0.1153	0.0839	0.0178	-0.0969	0.1188	0.0283	-0.1153	0.1188	0.0213
	Greece	-0.0555	0.0603	0.0145	-0.1532	0.1320	0.0306	-0.1532	0.1320	0.0204
	Hungary	-0.0846	0.0781	0.0190	-0.2108	0.2450	0.0412	-0.2108	0.2450	0.0272
	Italy	-0.0820	0.0493	0.0133	-0.1096	0.1198	0.0299	-0.1096	0.1198	0.0195
	Poland	-0.0714	0.0520	0.0154	-0.1494	0.1352	0.0325	-0.1494	0.1352	0.0218
	Spain	-0.0650	0.0574	0.0129	-0.1271	0.1239	0.0282	-0.1271	0.1239	0.0186
	Sweden	-0.1104	0.0826	0.0175	-0.1107	0.1320	0.0341	-0.1107	0.1320	0.0234
	Switzerland	-0.1004	0.0752	0.0138	-0.1069	0.0865	0.0221	-0.1069	0.0865	0.0166
	UK	-0.0824	0.0610	0.0125	-0.1045	0.1399	0.0282	-0.1045	0.1399	0.0183
East Asia	Hong Kong	-0.0426	0.0471	0.0124	-0.1724	0.1358	0.0312	-0.1724	0.1358	0.0196
	Indonesia	-0.1522	0.0628	0.0202	-0.2006	0.1497	0.0342	-0.2006	0.1497	0.0249
	Japan	-0.0894	0.0633	0.0157	-0.0829	0.1127	0.0213	-0.0894	0.1127	0.0175
	Malaysia	-0.0576	0.0458	0.0097	-0.0981	0.0536	0.0177	-0.0981	0.0536	0.0125
	Taiwan	-0.0831	0.0841	0.0177	-0.0856	0.0975	0.0267	-0.0856	0.0975	0.0206
	Thailand	-0.1280	0.0641	0.0183	-0.1479	0.1037	0.0255	-0.1479	0.1037	0.0206
	South Korea	-0.1054	0.1054	0.0263	-0.2123	0.2094	0.0401	-0.2123	0.2094	0.0308
Latin America	Argentina	-0.3327	0.2340	0.0308	-0.1877	0.1077	0.0316	-0.3327	0.2340	0.0310
	Brazil	-0.1243	0.1295	0.0288	-0.2104	0.1840	0.0439	-0.2104	0.1840	0.0337
	Chile	-0.0421	0.0370	0.0111	-0.1180	0.1059	0.0235	-0.1180	0.1059	0.0156
	Mexico	-0.0723	0.0827	0.0173	-0.1695	0.1368	0.0338	-0.1695	0.1368	0.0232
Other	China	-0.0866	0.1035	0.0173	-0.0882	0.1196	0.0287	-0.0882	0.1196	0.0211
	India	-0.1341	0.0762	0.0181	-0.1583	0.2060	0.0359	-0.1583	0.2060	0.0245
	Israel	-0.0904	0.0914	0.0165	-0.1187	0.0940	0.0263	-0.1187	0.0940	0.0197
	Russia	-0.0943	0.0991	0.0226	-0.2535	0.2296	0.0446	-0.2535	0.2296	0.0305

This table presents the summary statistics (minimum, maximum and standard deviation) of two-day stock market returns for the full sample period, the pre-crisis period and the crisis period. We use the Lehman Brothers bankruptcy filing date as the crisis "point" (September 15th, 2008) in order to divide the full sample into the two sub-samples: pre-crisis period and crisis period. Countries are grouped by region.

Table 5. Test of Contagion (Lehman Brothers Crisis Point)

	Full Period		Pre-crisis Period		Crisis Period					
	N =	1964	N =	1747	N =	217	Test Statistic		Contagion?	
Country	r_U	r_A	r_U	r_A	r_U	r_A	t_U	t_A	t_U	t_A
Australia	0.31	0.19	0.11	0.07	0.58	0.39	4.72	3.00	Y	Y
Canada	0.70	0.50	0.59	0.40	0.81	0.63	3.45	2.59	Y	Y
France	0.62	0.42	0.54	0.35	0.72	0.52	2.44	1.71	Y	Y
Germany	0.65	0.45	0.58	0.38	0.76	0.56	3.00	2.15	Y	Y
Greece	0.35	0.21	0.19	0.11	0.53	0.35	3.27	2.07	Y	Y
Hungary	0.36	0.22	0.17	0.10	0.54	0.35	3.20	2.03	Y	Y
Italy	0.57	0.38	0.48	0.31	0.66	0.46	2.05	1.40	Y	N
Poland	0.34	0.21	0.17	0.10	0.53	0.35	3.43	2.17	Y	Y
Spain	0.56	0.37	0.43	0.27	0.69	0.49	3.00	2.05	Y	Y
Sweden	0.55	0.36	0.47	0.30	0.63	0.43	1.68	1.13	Y	N
Switzerland	0.54	0.35	0.45	0.28	0.66	0.45	2.59	1.73	Y	Y
UK	0.48	0.31	0.48	0.31	0.72	0.52	5.46	3.71	Y	Y
Hong Kong	0.17	0.10	0.17	0.10	0.53	0.35	5.89	3.66	Y	Y
Indonesia	0.10	0.06	0.10	0.06	0.29	0.18	2.79	1.67	Y	Y
Japan	0.11	0.07	0.11	0.07	0.19	0.11	1.11	0.66	N	N
Malaysia	0.06	0.03	0.06	0.03	0.33	0.21	4.02	2.43	Y	Y
Taiwan	0.16	0.10	0.16	0.10	0.36	0.22	2.99	1.80	Y	Y
Thailand	0.09	0.06	0.09	0.06	0.50	0.32	6.28	3.87	Y	Y
South Korea	0.23	0.14	0.13	0.08	0.45	0.29	3.58	2.20	Y	Y
Argentina	0.39	0.24	0.23	0.14	0.70	0.51	6.49	4.36	Y	Y
Brazil	0.61	0.41	0.48	0.30	0.81	0.63	6.09	4.42	Y	Y
Chile	0.51	0.33	0.35	0.22	0.73	0.53	5.05	3.48	Y	Y
Mexico	0.71	0.51	0.62	0.42	0.83	0.65	4.04	3.04	Y	Y
China	0.05	0.03	-0.01	0.00	0.17	0.10	1.68	0.99	Y	N

Table 5. Continued

Country	Full Period		Pre-crisis Period		Crisis Period		Test Statistic		Contagion?	
	N =	1964	N =	1747	N =	217				
	r_U	r_A	r_U	r_A	r_U	r_A	t_U	t_A	t_U	t_A
India	0.28	0.17	0.11	0.07	0.49	0.32	3.52	2.19	Y	Y
Israel	0.34	0.21	0.27	0.16	0.48	0.31	2.29	1.43	Y	N
Russia	0.28	0.17	0.17	0.10	0.40	0.25	1.91	1.17	Y	N
TOTAL									26	21

This table presents the main results of the study. It shows the unadjusted (r_U) and adjusted (r_A) correlation coefficients for the full sample period, the pre-crisis period, and the crisis period. We use the Lehman Brothers bankruptcy filing date as the crisis "point" (September 15th, 2008) in order to divide the full sample into the two sub-samples: pre-crisis period and crisis period. The test of contagion is also presented. A country that has suffered from contagion is indicated by a "Y" under the column labeled "Contagion?". t_U refers to the t-statistic to test for contagion using the unadjusted correlation coefficients, and t_A refers to the t-statistics to test for contagion using adjusted correlation coefficients. Countries are grouped by region. The group includes only OECD countries, the second group includes Latin American countries, the third group includes the East Asian countries, and the fourth group includes the emerging markets. The last row shows the total number of countries that suffered from contagion under each test: unadjusted and adjusted correlation coefficients.

Table 6. Test of Contagion (Bear Stearns & Co. Crisis Point)

Country	Full Period		Pre-crisis Period		Crisis Period		Test Statistic		Contagion?	
	N =	1964	N =	1415	N =	549				
	r_U	r_A	r_U	r_A	r_U	r_A	t_U	t_A	t_U	t_A
Australia	0.31	0.22	0.09	0.06	0.46	0.33	3.57	2.54	Y	Y
Canada	0.70	0.56	0.61	0.47	0.76	0.62	2.38	1.92	Y	Y
France	0.62	0.48	0.55	0.41	0.67	0.53	1.80	1.39	Y	N

Table 6. Continued

	Full Period		Pre-crisis Period		Crisis Period					
	N =	1964	N =	1415	N =	549	Test Statistic		Contagion?	
Country	r_U	r_A	r_U	r_A	r_U	r_A	t_U	t_A	t_U	t_A
Germany	0.65	0.50	0.62	0.47	0.69	0.54	1.45	1.13	N	N
Greece	0.35	0.24	0.18	0.12	0.45	0.33	2.57	1.83	Y	Y
Hungary	0.36	0.25	0.12	0.08	0.50	0.36	3.56	2.55	Y	Y
Italy	0.57	0.43	0.50	0.36	0.63	0.48	1.73	1.31	Y	N
Poland	0.34	0.24	0.16	0.11	0.45	0.32	2.81	1.99	Y	Y
Spain	0.56	0.42	0.44	0.32	0.63	0.48	2.27	1.72	Y	Y
Sweden	0.55	0.41	0.47	0.34	0.60	0.45	1.43	1.07	N	N
Switzerland	0.54	0.40	0.45	0.32	0.61	0.46	2.15	1.60	Y	N
UK	0.47	0.34	0.47	0.34	0.68	0.53	6.67	5.02	Y	Y
Hong Kong	0.18	0.12	0.18	0.12	0.44	0.31	5.91	4.13	Y	Y
Indonesia	0.07	0.05	0.07	0.05	0.27	0.19	4.22	2.88	Y	Y
Japan	0.13	0.09	0.13	0.09	0.15	0.10	0.45	0.31	N	N
Malaysia	0.05	0.03	0.05	0.03	0.22	0.15	3.58	2.45	Y	Y
Taiwan	0.17	0.12	0.17	0.12	0.27	0.18	2.08	1.42	Y	N
Thailand	0.09	0.06	0.09	0.06	0.41	0.29	7.15	4.96	Y	Y
South Korea	0.23	0.16	0.13	0.09	0.37	0.26	3.21	2.23	Y	Y
Argentina	0.39	0.28	0.20	0.13	0.65	0.51	7.66	5.68	Y	Y
Brazil	0.61	0.46	0.45	0.32	0.76	0.62	5.88	4.62	Y	Y
Chile	0.51	0.37	0.32	0.23	0.62	0.47	3.45	2.57	Y	Y
Mexico	0.71	0.56	0.59	0.44	0.79	0.66	3.97	3.24	Y	Y

Table 6. Continued

	Full Period		Pre-crisis Period		Crisis Period					
	N =	1964	N =	1415	N =	549	Test Statistic		Contagion?	
Country	r_U	r_A	r_U	r_A	r_U	r_A	t_U	t_A	t_U	t_A
China	0.05	0.03	0.02	0.01	0.07	0.05	0.57	0.39	N	N
India	0.28	0.19	0.09	0.06	0.40	0.29	2.87	2.01	Y	Y
Israel	0.34	0.24	0.23	0.16	0.46	0.33	2.85	2.03	Y	Y
Russia	0.28	0.19	0.16	0.11	0.37	0.26	2.07	1.44	Y	N
TOTAL									23	18

This table presents the main results of the study. It shows the unadjusted (r_U) and adjusted (r_A) correlation coefficients for the full sample period, the pre-crisis period, and the crisis period. We use the Bear Stearns redemptions halt date as the crisis "point" (June 7th, 2007) in order to divide the full sample into the two sub-samples: pre-crisis period and crisis period. The test of contagion is also presented. A country that has suffered from contagion is indicated by a "Y" under the column labeled "Contagion?". t_U refers to the t-statistic to test for contagion using the unadjusted correlation coefficients, and t_A refers to the t-statistics to test for contagion using adjusted correlation coefficients. Countries are grouped by region. The group includes only OECD countries, the second group includes Latin American countries, the third group includes the East Asian countries, and the fourth group includes the emerging markets. The last row shows the total number of countries that suffered from contagion under each test: unadjusted and adjusted correlation coefficients.

Several patterns are immediately apparent. The highest correlation coefficients for the full period occur between two expected pairs of countries. Canada and the U.S. are highly correlated with a coefficient of 0.5. Mexico and the U.S. are also highly correlated (0.51). Other countries with a stock market highly correlated to that of the U.S. are most of the European countries such as Spain, Sweden, Italy, Switzerland, France and Germany. Furthermore, the U.S. shows higher stock market correlation with Latin American countries than with East Asian countries.[1]

Comparing the crisis period adjusted correlation coefficient to those from the pre-crisis period, we see a sizable increase in the numbers. Countries such as Greece, Hungary, Poland, Indonesia, Thailand, Argentina and India show a post-shock correlation coefficient that is 3 or more times greater than its pre-crisis counterpart. Malaysia's correlation to the U.S. market increased six-fold after the shock. Our test of contagion, however, consists of any significant increase in the crisis correlation coefficient relative to the full period as shown in equation (13). Surprisingly, we find that most countries evaluated here have suffered from contagion during the recent financial crisis. 21 out of 27 countries show evidence of contagion as measured by the heteroskedasticity-adjusted correlation coefficients. All Latin American economies, as well as all East Asian economies (with the exception of Japan), suffered from contagion. It is also important to note that Japan is the only country with no evidence of contagion whether we use the adjusted or unadjusted coefficients. Also, there are significantly less cases of contagion if we use the adjusted correlation coefficient (21 versus 26), which indicates the importance of accounting for the increase in market volatility in the crisis country after the shock.

Table 6 shows the results of our contagion tests when we identify the crisis triggering event as June 7th, 2007. The results show evidence of significant international financial contagion. In fact, the results are very similar to those shown in Table 5. There are 3 less cases of contagion in this set of results. Israel appears to have suffered from contagion after Bear Stearns & Co. halted redemptions from its two funds, but it does not show any evidence of contagion after the Lehman Brothers bankruptcy filing. On the other hand, France, Germany, Switzerland and Taiwan show no evidence of contagion after June 7th, 2007, but appear to have suffered from contagion after September 15th, 2008. Overall, our results are very similar across crisis-triggering events and there is significant evidence of contagion during the recent financial crisis. These results

[1] Brazil has a coefficient of 0.41 and Chile has a coefficient of 0.33, while the highest correlation coefficient for the East Asian countries is only 0.14 in the case of South Korea.

are highly in contrast with the more recent literature on the crises of the 1990s.[2] Forbes and Rigobon (2002) show that after adjusting for heteroskedasticity in market returns, there is very little evidence of contagion. Therefore, they argue that the spread of a crisis across markets is mainly due to interdependence or normal cross-market economic activity. Having answered our first question, we turn our attention to the factors determining the spread of a crisis via contagion.

The significant evidence of cross-country contagion will allow us to shed some light on the pre-crisis economic conditions which make a country more prone to suffer from contagion. In section V(a), we ranked the sampled countries using three pre-crisis criteria: (1) the country's macroeconomic similarity with the U.S. economy, (2) the country's economic condition, and (3) the country's degree of dependence on real links. Based on these rankings (see Table 2) and our evidence of contagion, we proceed to answer our second question.

De Gregorio and Valdes (2000) find that during the debt crisis of 1982, the Asian crisis of 1997 and the Mexican 1994 devaluation, exchange rate flexibility and debt maturity structure tilted towards long-term significantly limit contagion measured by complements of country credit ratings. Although these findings are very relevant, particularly for policy reform, our approach is different. We simply attempt to reveal which pre-crisis economic conditions make a country more likely to be infected by an external crisis. Contrasting our three economic measures developed in section V(a) to our contagion test results, we find that macroeconomic similarities across countries are a significant factor in identifying the vulnerability of a country to contagion. In fact, we find that 8 out of the 10 countries that did *not* suffer from contagion had pre-crisis economies that were very dissimilar to that of the United States. Five of the countries *not* infected are in the bottom 25% when ranked by the macroeconomic similarity index (MS_j). Three countries are in the bottom 50% indicated by a Q3 in Table 2. This suggests that having macroeconomic characteristics that are similar to that of the crisis country before the shock increases the likelihood of contagion. Therefore, investors tend to react excessively in countries that are economically similar to the crisis country. In other words, investors behave negatively towards countries with similar economies to the crisis country, regardless of whether these countries are economically sound and/or have a high dependence on real (trade and financial) links.

The other two criteria (EC_j and DEP_j) do not show the strong pattern shown by the macroeconomic similarity index. There is no discernible pattern for these variables. This suggests that the economic health of a country before the crisis is

---

[2] The literature on contagion has been primarily focused on three main crises: the Tequila crisis, the Asian Flu, and the Russian Debt crisis.

not a factor that drives investors to react excessively. Furthermore, a high dependence on goods and services and financial trade does not lead investors to expect a country to be infected by the crisis. In summary, our evidence shows that only macroeconomic similarities drive investors to expect the spread of a crisis. Therefore, as investors act on these expectations by selling assets in these soon-to-be-affected markets, these markets also suffer a negative shock as their expectations become self-fulfilling.

VI. Robustness Tests of Contagion

In this section we perform an extensive series of sensitivity tests. We test for the impact of modifying the frequency of returns, the period definitions, the lag structure of the VAR model and the currency denomination. Overall, the central results do not change significantly. Table 7 shows the results from our sensitivity tests.

Table 7. Robustness Tests

Crisis Point	Currency of Returns	Return Frequency	Lags Included	Cases of Contagion	
				r_U	r_A
9/15/2008	USD	Daily	1	21	13
9/15/2008	USD	Daily	5	24	17
9/15/2008	USD	2-day avg.	1	26	20
9/15/2008	Local	Daily	1	20	13
9/15/2008	Local	Daily	5	23	16
9/15/2008	Local	2-day avg.	1	25	17
9/15/2008	Local	2-day avg.	5	25	17
6/7/2007	USD	Daily	1	21	15
6/7/2007	USD	Daily	5	21	17
6/7/2007	USD	2-day avg.	1	23	20
6/7/2007	Local	Daily	1	21	12
6/7/2007	Local	Daily	5	22	14
6/7/2007	Local	2-day avg.	1	24	18
6/7/2007	Local	2-day avg.	5	22	14

This table presents the results from the robustness tests. We performed the tests of contagion under 14 different specifications which alter the return currency denomination (USD or local currency), frequency of returns (daily or 2-day average returns) and the number of lags included in the vector autoregressive model (1 or 5 lags). We only show the number of cases of contagion under each test for each type of correlation coefficient: unadjusted (r_U) and adjusted (r_A).

To conserve space, we only show the number of cases of contagion we find under each set of specifications analyzed. For example, when we use the *local currency* of the countries to construct *daily* returns using only *1 lag* in the VAR model, we find that 13 out of 27 countries suffer from contagion after the Lehman Brothers bankruptcy filing.

In the base analysis results shown in Table 5 and Table 6, we find a greater number of cases of contagion than in our sensitivity tests (the average number of cases of contagion in Table 7 is approximately 16). The main result of this chapter still holds, however. We find very significant evidence of contagion across countries resulting from the recent U.S. financial crisis.

CONCLUSION

In order to better understand the underpinnings of cross-country crisis propagation, this chapter studies the recent financial crisis in an attempt to answer two related questions. First, can the recent shock transmission from the U.S. to a variety of countries be explained by contagion or investors' excessive behavior, or is the transmission purely due to real links between countries. Formally defining contagion as the transmission of a shock from the crisis market to other markets due to the intensification of behavioral linkages in excess of what is warranted by the pre-crisis economic conditions, we measure contagion using a popular statistical method. Bias-adjusted correlation coefficients were calculated for our full sample and for a sub-sample covering only the post-shock period. Any increase in these correlation coefficients was used as evidence of contagion. In contrast with the recent literature on contagion, we find significant evidence of contagion from the U.S. to a wide spectrum of countries.

The second question we address in this chapter is the issue of what pre-crisis economic characteristics make a country more likely to be infected by a crisis occurring elsewhere. We proposed three economic criteria to help answer this question: (1) the country's macroeconomic similarity with the U.S. economy, (2) the country's economic condition, and (3) the country's degree of dependence on real links. These economic conditions are quantified using macroeconomic data for all the countries sampled. By matching these macroeconomic data to our results from the tests of contagion, we find that contagion occurs to countries that have strong pre-crisis macroeconomic similarities to the crisis country. The pre-crisis economic state of the country and its dependence on cross-country linkages (trade and financial) do not affect the likelihood of contagion.

Although this chapter provides a comprehensive study of contagion during the recent financial crisis, there is much room for further research. An interesting study would entail identifying those countries not affected by the recent crisis (such as Italy, Sweden, Japan, China and Russia according to our findings) and exploring their characteristics in order to understand contagion or the lack of it in more detail. Also, the importance of microeconomic and institutional factors in propagating shocks has not been explored extensively. Researching these factors could prove very enlightening, as it has been in other areas such as foreign exchange rate determination. Finally, a larger sample of countries could be examined. Fortunately, it appears as if the field has had and will have a variety of cases to investigate given that the era of economic crises does not seem to be over.

References

Calvo, Guillermo, and Enrique Mendoza, 1998, Rational contagion and the globalization of security markets, (University of Maryland).

Calvo, Sarah, and Graciela M. Reinhart, 1996, Capital flows to Latin America: Is there any evidence of contagion effects?, in Guillermo A. Calvo, Morris Goldstein, and Eduard Hochreiter, eds.: *Private capital flows to emerging markets after the Mexican crisis* (Institute for International Economics, Washington, DC).

Claessens, Stijn, Rudiger W. Dornbusch, and Yung Chul Park, 2001, Contagion: Why crises spread and how this can be stopped, in Stijn Claessens, and Kristin J. Forbes, eds.: *International financial contagion* (Kluwer Academic Publishers, Boston).

Claessens, Stijn, and Kristin J. Forbes, eds., 2001. *International financial contagion* (Kluwer Academic Publishers, Boston).

Eichengreen, Barry, and Andrew Rose, 1999, Contagious currency crisis: Channels of conveyance, in T. Ito, and A. Krueger, eds.: *Changes in exchange rate in rapidly developing countries: Theory, practice, and policy issues* (University of Chicago Press, Chicago).

Forbes, Kristin J., 2004, The Asian flu and Russian virus: Firm-level evidence on how crises are transmitted internationally, *Journal of International Economics* 63, 59-92.

Forbes, Kristin J., and Menzie D. Chinn, 2004, A decomposition of global linkages in financial markets over time, *The Review of Economic and Statistics* 86, 705-722.

Forbes, Kristin J., and Roberto Rigobon, 2001, Measuring contagion: Conceptual and empirical issues, in Stijn Claessens, and Kristin J. Forbes, eds.: *International financial contagion* (Kluwer Academic Publishers, Boston).

Forbes, Kristin J., and Roberto Rigobon, 2002, No contagion, only interdependence: Measuring stock market comovements, *Journal of Finance* 57, 2223-2261.

Gregorio, Jose De, and Rodrigo O. Valdes, 2001, Crisis transmission: Evidence from the debt, tequila, and Asian flu crisis, in Stijn Claessens, and Kristin J. Forbes, eds.: *International financial contagion* (Kluwer Academic Publishers, Boston).

Krugman, Paul, 2009. *The return of depression economics and the crisis of 2008* (W.W. Norton & Company Inc., New Work).

Pritsker, Matt, 2001, The channels for financial contagion, in Stijn Claessens, and Kristin J. Forbes, eds.: *International financial contagion* (Kluwer Academic Publishers, Boston).

Reinhart, Carmen, and Graciela Kaminsky, 1998, On crises, contagion, and confusion, (Munich Personal RePEe Archive).

In: Financial Crisis in the Global ...
Editors: A. Tomohara, M. Sherlock
ISBN: 978-1-61470-597-0

Chapter 5

CONTAGION OF BANKING AND CURRENCY CRISES

Kenshi Taketa*
School of International Politics, Economics & Communication
Aoyama Gakuin University, 4-4-25 Shibuya Shibuya-ku
Tokyo 150-8366, Japan

Abstract

I construct a micro-model of contagious twin crises (banking crises and currency crises). I consider a situation where (1) banks in each country do not have any interbank deposits and (2) countries do not have a common lender. The model shows that financial crises can spread across countries even in this situation due to the learning behavior of international investors. Moreover, the model clarifies (1) the timing of financial crises, (2) the distinction between accidental simultaneous occurrences of financial crises and contagion of financial crises, and (3) the timing of contagion. The model shows that there are three types of contagion in terms of dynamics: (1) contemporaneous contagion, (2) lagged contagion and (3) forward contagion. The first type of contagion occurs when a financial crisis in one country spreads to another country in the same time period. The second type occurs when a financial crisis in one country spreads to another country in a subsequent period. The third type occurs when an anticipated financial crisis in one country spreads to another country prior to the original crisis' onset.

---

*E-mail address: ktaketa@sipeb.aoyama.ac.jp

Keywords: Contagion; Banking Crises; Currency Crises; Global Game

JEL Classifications: F31; E58; D82; C72

1. Introduction

A commonly held view of financial crises is that they tend to be regional and contagious. They begin locally, in some region, country, or institution, and subsequently spread elsewhere. There are many examples of contagious financial crises in recent years: the Mexican Debt crisis in 1982, the Mexican *Tequila* effect in December of 1994, the Asian *Flu* in the last half of 1997, the Russian *Virus* in August of 1998, the Brazilian *Sneeze* in January of 1999, the NASDAQ *Rash* in April of 2000, and so on. Clearly, the names of these financial crises capture the view that they are contagious. This chapter studies why such contagion happens.

The seminal paper about financial crises is Diamond and Dybvig (1983), which shows that bank runs can arise as a Nash equilibrium. If a depositor thinks that every other depositor will withdraw their money in the near future, she will likewise decide to withdraw — leading to a bank run. Therefore, bank runs have a kind of self-fulfilling property: they can occur simply because many depositors think they will. The Diamond and Dybvig model (the DD model) is often referred to as the theoretical basis for financial panics.

This chapter extends the DD model to study a contagion channel, called a wake-up call effect, by which a country-specific crisis can be transmitted to other countries. Moreover, this chapter deals with currency crises explicitly, something omitted from the DD model. In this chapter, the key to explaining contagion in financial crises lies in the learning behavior of international investors. To understand this behavior, consider two countries, country A and country B. Suppose a financial crisis happens in country A. It often leads to a recession in country A. As long as the economic fundamentals in country A correlate with those in country B, the recession in country A could indicate something about (have some effects on) the economic fundamentals in country B. In that case, the behavior of investors who invest in country B may (or may not) be conditional on the financial crisis in country A. That is, investors who invest in country B may (or may not) learn some information about country B from the financial crisis in country A, which can trigger a similar financial crisis in country B. This chapter clarifies (1) the timing of financial crises, (2) the distinction between coincidence of financial crises and contagion of financial crises, and (3) the timing of contagion. A dynamic aspect of contagion (the timing of contagion) has not been investigated so far in detail. This chapter shows that there are three types of contagion in terms of dynamics: (1) contemporaneous contagion, (2) lagged contagion, and (3) forward contagion. The first type of contagion occurs when a financial crisis in one country spreads to another country in the same time period. The second type occurs when a financial crisis in one country in a period spreads to another country in a subsequent time period. The third type occurs when an anticipated financial crisis in one country spreads to another country prior to the original crisis' onset.

This chapter is organized as follows. In Section 2., I review the literature. In Section 3., I present a micro-model to explain contagion of financial crises due to the learning behavior of the international investors. I conclude in Section 4.. Proofs are presented in Appendix.

2. Related Literature

An extensive literature has explored how financial crises are transmitted internationally.[1]

A channel by which a country-specific crisis can be transmitted to other countries is through a wake-up call effect. The basic idea is that a crisis in one country can provide information about other countries. For example, if a country with specific macroeconomic characteristics such as a weak banking sector is discovered to be susceptible to a currency crisis, then investors will reassess the risk of other countries with similar macroeconomic fundamentals. Eichengreen et al. (1996) argue that this wake-up call effect is empirically significant. Relating to this reassessment of macroeconomic fundamentals, Furman and Stiglitz (1998), Tornell (1999), Krugman (1999) and Masson (1999a, b) argue that contagion can be explained as jumps between multiple equilibria. However, it is often pointed out that multiple equilibria models of crises provide only a feeble explanation of contagion, as they are consistent with other outcomes, including the absence of contagion. Moreover, even if a crisis occurs in two countries, it may be a coincidence. In multiple equilibria models, it is not very clear whether or not the crisis in one country in fact triggers the crisis in the other, as these models do not sufficiently explain the mechanism for transition between multi-

[1]For an excellent survey, see Forbes (2004).

ple equilibria.

In contrast with these models, this chapter uses the "Global Game Approach" proposed by Morris and Shin (1998). They propose methods of equilibrium refinement which can be used to explain the wake-up call effect. This approach enables us to explain how and why a particular equilibrium can be selected. Using this type of equilibrium refinement technique, one can provide a new explanation for contagion. An important difference between Morris and Shin (1998) and this chapter is that I focus on the issue contagion directly using methods not originally intended for this purpose.

3. The Model

In many financial crises, two empirical facts are often observed. The first is that financial crises are correlated with a recession (i.e., poor economic fundamentals).[2] The second is that currency crises tend to occur with banking crises, called "twin crises".[3] In this section, I construct a micro model to capture these empirical facts.

There are two countries: country A and country B. Ex ante, the two are identical. These two countries are interrelated thorough some economic mechanism such as trade. For each country, there are four classes of players: international investors, a central bank, commercial banks, and domestic firms. International investors invest their money in commercial banks in one of the countries. In this investment, the central bank exchanges the invested money (which is the foreign currency) into the domestic currency at some exchange rate. The commercial banks lend the money to the domestic firms. The domestic firms earn some revenues by using the lent money and repay the commercial banks out of their revenues. Then the commercial banks repay the international investors. In this repayment, the central bank exchanges the domestic currency into the foreign currency at some exchange rate.

3.1. Preferences

There are two sets of international investors. One is the set of investors who deposit in country A (call this the set A), and the other is the set of investors

[2]See Frankel and Rose (1996).

[3]See Kaminsky and Reinhart (1998) and Goldstein et al. (2000).

who deposit in country B (call this the set B). Assume the sets are disjoint. There are three periods (0, 1, 2). Each agent has an endowment of one unit and deposits it in one of the countries in period 0. Agents face private (uninsurable) liquidity shocks: they need either to consume in period 1 (impatient) or in period 2 (patient).

$$U = \begin{cases} u(c_1) & \text{with probability } w \\ u(c_2) & \text{with probability } 1-w \end{cases}, \tag{1}$$

where $u(\cdot)$ is utility function ($u'(\cdot) > 0$, $u''(\cdot) < 0$), c_t is consumption in period t ($t = 1, 2$) and w is some known constant ($0 < w < 1$).

In period 0, they do not know whether they are patient or not. At the beginning of period 1, they learn this information. "Impatient" corresponds to the situation where they need money in period 1 while "patient" corresponds to the situation where they need money in period 2.

3.2. Banks and Demand Deposits

In each country, there is a central bank and a representative competitive commercial bank. The central bank acts as an intermediary for transaction of domestic currency and foreign currency. When the international investors withdraw their money from the commercial bank, the central bank has to exchange the domestic currency and the foreign currency at some exchange rate.[4]

The commercial banks borrow money from the international investors and lend to the domestic firms. I will not investigate the profit-earning behavior of the domestic firms in detail. For simplicity, I assume the repayment of the domestic firms can be summarized into "assets" from the viewpoint of lenders as follows. There are two classes of "assets" available to the banks. One is a safe and liquid storage technology with a low (unit) gross rate of return. Another is a risky and illiquid asset with high-expected return. One unit stored at period t produces one unit at period $t + 1$. As for the risky asset, its return, $R_i(t)$, is given by:

$$R_i(t) = \begin{cases} r & \text{at } t = 1 \;\; (0 < r \leq 1) \\ R(\theta_i) & \text{at } t = 2 \end{cases}, \tag{2}$$

where t is the time of liquidation, $R(\theta_i)$ is any increasing differentiable function of θ_i, and θ_i is a random variable with a differentiable density $g(\theta_i)$ and a corresponding cumulative distribution function, $G(\theta_i)$. I assume $Supp(\theta_i) = [L, U]$.

[4]The determination of the exchange rate will be explained in detail below.

θ_i indexes some underlying "economic fundamentals" of country i related to the assets of the commercial banks ($i = A, B$). I assume the economic fundamentals of country A are positively correlated to those of country B (i.e., $Cov(\theta_A, \theta_B) > 0$). Note that the returns of risky assets liquidated in period 1 are not greater than the returns of the safe assets.

I think of θ_i as some "goodness" of country i from the viewpoint of the international investors. The higher θ_i is, the better (i.e. the more "profitable") the country is from the viewpoint of the international investors. For example, it is typical to think that high economic growth, stable prices, and positive trade balances are good. I assume that $E_{\theta_i}[u(R(\theta_i))] > u(1)$: the risky asset yields a higher expected payoff if held until period 2.

In period 1, the central bank of country i has foreign reserves RX_{i1}, which is an endowment for the central bank. In period 2, the central bank receives foreign reserves as a result of economic activities of the domestic firms. In particular, I assume the central bank receives foreign reserves ($RX_{i2}(\theta_i)$) that depend positively on θ_i. It suggests that as economic fundamentals improve, the country can increase its foreign reserves. The central bank is assumed to set the exchange rate $e_t = 1$ whenever possible. This means that $e_1 = e_2 = 1$ when the central bank is successful in pegging the exchange rate. On the other hand, $e_t > 1$ if the central bank fails to peg, which results in a devaluation of the domestic currency. That is, I measure the exchange rate so that a larger value means depreciation. For simplicity, I call this devaluation a currency crisis.[5]

Definition 1 (Currency Crisis)**.** A currency crisis is defined as $e_t > 1$.

The commercial bank offers the international investors demand deposit contracts. Demand deposit contracts offer conversion of deposits into cash at par on demand in period 1 conditional on sufficient cash being available. If, however, sufficient cash is not available, then the contract specifies that the bank will liquidate its portfolio and then evenly divide its assets amongst depositors that choose to exit. At this point in time, the bank goes out of business. For those depositors who choose to keep their assets in the bank until period 2, the bank promises to pay a stochastic amount, which is contingent upon the returns on the bank's assets and the proportion of early withdrawal, unless a bank run occurs in period 1.[6]

[5] The DD model has not dealt with the exchange rate.

[6] In this model, I will not investigate the optimal contract between the bank and depositors. In

3.3. Information Structure

In this section I construct an information structure of the baseline model that is an extension of the DD model. As becomes clear later, the information structure is critical in the explanation of contagious financial crises in my model.

At first, in period 0, the international investors deposit their endowment in a commercial bank in one of the countries. The commercial banks invest their money in both safe and risky domestic firms.

In period 1, nature selects at random (and with equal probability) one of the sets of international investors to receive information about their bank and to act. Let's call the country in which they have invested the first country. Information is received in the form of private signals about the underlying economic fundamentals of the country in which they have invested. Suppose country i is selected first. Depositor j of country i receives a private signal $x_{j,i} = \theta_i + \epsilon_{j,i}$, where $\epsilon_{j,i}$ is independent and identically distributed across j. For simplicity, assume that $\epsilon_{j,i}$ is distributed uniformly on $[-\epsilon, \epsilon]$. Note that private signals themselves are correlated among depositors in the same set of international investors because every signal shares a common θ_i. This is true even though the noise $\epsilon_{j,i}$ is independent and identically distributed across j. Therefore each depositor can "guess" the private signals of other depositors to some degree, conditional on his own private signal. Shortly thereafter, depositor h of another country $-i$ receives a private signal about country $-i$ with some idiosyncratic noise: $x_{h,-i} = \theta_{-i} + \epsilon_{h,-i}$, where $\epsilon_{h,-i}$ is independent and identically distributed across h. Again, assume that $\epsilon_{h,-i}$ is distributed uniformly on $[-\epsilon, \epsilon]$. $\epsilon_{j,i}$ and $\epsilon_{h,-i}$ are independent. Before acting, the depositors who move second learn what has happened in the first country.

In period 2, the economic fundamentals θ_A and θ_B are realized. Subsequently residual international investors claims in each country are settled.

Thus, the timing of this game can be described as follows.

- Period 0
  - International investors deposit their endowments in one of the countries.
  - Commercial banks invest a fraction of w of their deposits in the safe assets and a fraction of $1 - w$ of their deposits in the risky assets.

---

particular, I am not solving for the optimal contractual form itself. Demand deposit contracts are standard contracts offered by the bank. I take them as given.

- Period 1
  - The international investors learn whether they are patient or impatient.
  - Nature chooses "the first country".
  - The international investors who deposit in country i (the first country) receive private signals, with some noise, about underlying economic fundamentals of country i.
  - The international investors who deposit in country i choose between two actions (to withdraw in period 1 or to wait until period 2).
  - The international investors who deposit in country i and demand early withdrawal are paid.
  - The international investors who deposit in country $-i$ learn what has happened in country i.
  - The international investors who deposit in country $-i$ receive private signals, with some noise, about underlying economic fundamentals of country $-i$.
  - The international investors who deposit in country $-i$ choose between two actions (to withdraw in period 1 or to wait until period 2).
  - The international investors who deposit in country $-i$ and demand early withdrawal are paid.
- Period 2
  - Economic fundamentals θ_A and θ_B are realized.
  - Residual international investors claims in each country are settled.

3.4. Payoff of International Investors

In this section, I investigate the payoff for the international investors.

First note that if agents (international investors) are impatient, they will withdraw in period 1 regardless of the actions of other agents. They have no strategic choice. But if agents are patient, they face a non-trivial binary choice: they can withdraw in period 1 or they can wait until period 2. Therefore, patient agents behave strategically conditional on the behavior of other agents. I outline their payoffs below.

In period 1, there is a mass $1 - w$ of patient agents in each of the set A and the set B. Let n_A be the proportion of patient depositors who choose to withdraw in period 1 in country A. Then the total demand for cash in country A is $w + n_A(1 - w)$. The bank has w in cash in period 1, which is the return from the safe asset. Clearly, it is not enough to repay $w + n_A(1 - w)$ if n_A is positive. The bank has $1 - w$ invested in the risky assets from which it can generate $r(1 - w)$ in cash in period 1 if all the risky assets are terminated.

Therefore, if $w + n_A(1 - w) > w + r(1 - w)$ holds, then the bank becomes insolvent and goes out of business, and divides up the proceeds of its liquidated asset portfolio equally amongst its claimants in period 1. The condition for insolvency is rewritten as $n_A > r$. In this case, there will be no repayment in period 2.

On the other hand, if $n_A \leq r$ holds, then the bank does not go out of business. In order to pay the proportion n_A early demands by patient depositors in period 1, the bank has to liquidate $(1 - w)\frac{n_A}{r}$ of the illiquid assets in period 1. Note that its original investment into the illiquid assets is $1 - w$, thus the remaining proceeds in period 2 will be $\{(1 - w) - (1 - w)\frac{n_A}{r}\}R(\theta_A)$. The proceeds will be divided among the remaining $(1 - w)(1 - n_A)$ patient depositors.

Taking the exchange rate into account, the payoffs of the patient depositors are as follows:

$$u_W(\theta_A, n_A) = \begin{cases} u\left(\dfrac{1}{e_{A1}}\right) & \text{if } n_A \leq r \\ u\left(\dfrac{w + (1 - w)r}{e_{A1}(w + n_A(1 - w))}\right) & \text{if } n_A > r \end{cases}, \tag{3}$$

$$u_R(\theta_A, n_A) = \begin{cases} u\left(\dfrac{(1 - w)(1 - \frac{n_A}{r})R(\theta_A)}{e_{A1}(1 - w)(1 - n_A)}\right) & \text{if } n_A \leq r \\ u\,(0) & \text{if } n_A > r \end{cases}. \tag{4}$$

(3) is the payoff of withdrawal in period 1 while (4) is the payoff of waiting until period 2. $n_A \leq r$ corresponds to the case that bank runs do not occur. Each patient agent will choose to withdraw in period 1 or to remain until period 2 to maximize his payoff, conditional on n_A.[7]

[7]The payoffs of international investors who deposit in country B are exactly similar to (3) and (4).

3.5. Determination of the Exchange Rate

Before analyzing the equilibrium, I need to figure out how the exchange rate e_{it} is determined. First, I investigate the determination of the exchange rate in period 1 (e_{i1}). Then, I investigate the determination of the exchange rate in period 2 (e_{i2}).

I assume the central bank in each country seeks to stabilize the exchange rate. In particular, I assume the central bank seeks to peg the exchange rate at $e_{it} = 1$ whenever possible. I call the failure of pegging ($e_{it} > 1$) a currency crisis.

The determination of the exchange rate depends on the quantity of deposits withdrawn in that period. If the withdrawal exceeds the foreign reserve, then the desired exchange rate cannot be sustained. Therefore, I will clarify the amount of withdrawals in detail and then to compare the withdrawals to the amount of foreign reserves.

In period 1, the total withdrawal is $w + (1 - w)n_i$, where w are withdrawals by impatient agents while $(1 - w)n_i$ are withdrawals by patient agents. Recall that the impatient agents will always withdraw in period 1 while the patient agents might not. So the minimum possible repayment of the bank to the agents in period 1 is w. Clearly, if the foreign reserve in period 1, RX_{i1}, is smaller than w, then domestic currency will devalue. For simplicity, I assume $RX_{i1} > w$ $(i = 1, 2)$, i.e., both the countries have enough foreign reserves to sustain $e_{i1} = 1$ in case of minimum repayment. On the other hand, the maximum possible repayment in period 1 is $w + (1 - w)r$, which is the case of bank runs. If $RX_{i1} \geq w + (1 - w)r$, then $e_{i1} = 1$ can be sustained. In this case, the currency crisis will not occur in period 1 even if every investor rushes to withdraw his money (a bank run occurs in that period). I assume $RX_{i1} < w + (1 - w)r$, which leads to a currency crisis in period 1 as every investor rushes to withdraw his money.[8] If $w < RX_{i1} < w + (1 - w)n_i$, the withdrawal in period 1 exceeds the foreign reserve, and the central bank cannot peg the exchange rate at $e_{i1} = 1$. We see here the incidence of twin crises. The exchange rate will be determined so as to equate the demand for and supply of foreign currency. The demand for foreign currency is the withdrawal in period 1; $w + (1 - w)n_i$. The supply of foreign currency is equal to the foreign reserves; RX_{i1}. So the exchange rate

[8]This assumption fits an empirical regularity of countries vulnerable to financial crises. See Chang and Velasco (2000).

will be determined as follows:

$$\frac{w + (1 - w)Min\{n_i, r\}}{e_{i1}} = RX_{i1} \text{ if } w < RX_{i1} < w + (1 - w)n_i. \quad (5)$$

Rearranging this yields:

$$e_{i1} = \frac{w + (1 - w)Min\{n_i, r\}}{RX_{i1}} \text{ if } w < RX_{i1} < w + (1 - w)n_i. \quad (6)$$

In sum, the exchange rate in period 1 can be written as:

$$e_{i1} = Max\left\{1, \frac{w + (1 - w)Min\{n_i, r\}}{RX_{i1}}\right\}. \quad (7)$$

Next, I investigate how the exchange rate in period 2, e_{i2}, is determined. As before, if the quantity withdrawn does not exceed the foreign reserves, then a currency crisis is avoided. On the other hand, if the withdrawal is greater than foreign reserves, then a currency crisis occurs. In that case, the exchange rate is determined so as to equate the total demand for foreign currency with the total supply. The total demand is simply the withdrawal quantity in period 2: $(1 - w)(1 - n_i)R(\theta_i)$. Denote the total demand for foreign currency in period 2 by $D(\theta_i)$. The total supply is equal to foreign reserves in period 2. The central bank's foreign reserves remaining from period 2 (if any) can be written as: $Max\{0, RX_{i1} - (w + (1 - w)n_i)\}$. The first term corresponds to the case that the central bank has used up its foreign reserves in period 1. The second term corresponds to the case that the central bank has some foreign reserves remaining from period 1. Moreover, the central bank will receive new foreign reserves from the economic activities of domestic firms in period 2. Each unit of the remaining (not liquidated) risky assets produces $RX_{i2}(\theta_i)$ units of the foreign currency (foreign reserves). We can measure the total amount of risky assets not liquidated in period 1 as $(1 - w)(1 - \frac{n_i}{r})$, leading to new foreign reserves of $(1 - w)(1 - \frac{n_i}{r})RX_{i2}(\theta_i)$. So the total supply of the foreign currency in period 2, $S(\theta_i)$, is the following:

$$S(\theta_i) = Max\{0, RX_{i1} - (w + (1 - w)n_i)\} + (1 - w)\left(1 - \frac{n_i}{r}\right)RX_{i2}(\theta_i). \quad (8)$$

So if $D(\theta_i) > S(\theta_1)$, the exchange rate is determined as follows:

$$\frac{D(\theta_1)}{e_{i2}} = S(\theta_i) \text{ if } D(\theta_i) > S(\theta_1). \quad (9)$$

Rearranging this yields:

$$e_{i2} = \frac{D(\theta_1)}{S(\theta_i)} > 1 \text{ if } D(\theta_i) > S(\theta_1). \tag{10}$$

Thus the exchange rate can be summarized as follows:

$$e_{i2} = Max\left\{1, \frac{D(\theta_1)}{S(\theta_i)}\right\}. \tag{11}$$

3.6. Equilibrium and Contagion

After having characterized how the exchange rate is determined in each period, I can now analyze the equilibrium in this game. As is well known, there are multiple equilibria in the DD model. Thus I apply the "Global Game Approach" proposed by Morris and Shin (1998) to select amongst multiple equilibria and thereby explain the wake-up call effect.[9] Global Game Approach allows a multiple equilibrium refinement, when private signals are noisy. This is the case for some of the economic fundamentals in this model. By applying this equilibrium refinement, it can be explained more clearly why contagion occurs. One of the contributions of this chapter is to study the contagion channel, called the wake-up call effect, whereas Morris and Shin (1998) is not concerned with the problem of contagion.

Since the strategy of the international investors is a binary choice (to withdraw in period 1 or to wait until period 2), the refined equilibrium strategy takes a particularly simple form: Each patient agent will choose to wait until period 2 if and only if their private signal $x_{j,i}$ is above some threshold value $x^*_{j,i}$. That is, the equilibrium strategy has a kind of monotonicity. Let's call this equilibrium strategy the monotone strategy and the equilibria characterized by the monotone strategy the monotone equilibria. I will look at a symmetric Bayesian Nash equilibrium in the sense that every patient agent follows the same monotone strategy (meaning that $x^*_{j,i} = x^*_i$ for all j).

At first, I characterize the equilibrium strategy of the international investors who deposit in country A. Next, I characterize the equilibrium strategy of the international investors who deposit in country B. Recall that the international investors who deposit in country B can observe what has happened in country

[9]Dasgupta (2004) and Goldstein and Pauzner (2005) apply the Global Game Approach to the DD model, but they are not concerned with the wake-up call effect or a currency crisis either.

A in period 1 prior to their own withdrawal decision.[10] Therefore, the international investors who deposit in country B can use their observation as information supplemental to their own private signal of θ_B. For example, suppose that many investors withdraw their money from country A in period 1. Under the monotone strategy, it means that many investors received private signals below the threshold value. It in turn means that the economic fundamentals of country A (θ_A) are likely to be bad (i.e., low θ_A). This is useful for the international investors who deposit in country B, because it provides additional information about the imperfectly observed quantity θ_B.[11] That is why the international investors who deposit in country B can use their observations of country A as information about θ_B.

It is clear from (3) and (4) that n_A is quite important for the patient depositors in deciding whether to withdraw in period 1 or to wait until period 2. Since the private signals are correlated within a country, each agent can guess the private signals of other agents, conditional on his own private signal. If all agents follow the monotone strategy, each agent can calculate the expected value of n_A for each θ_A. Obviously, n_A will depend on the threshold value x_A^* and the true value θ_A under the monotone strategy. I denote $n_A = n(\theta_A, x_A^*)$. $n(\theta_A, x_A^*)$ can be calculated as follows.

Lemma 1 (Expected value of $n_A = n(\theta_A, x_A^*)$ conditional on θ_A). *Suppose all patient depositors follow the monotone strategy with the threshold value x_A^*. Then for any θ_A, each agent believes that a proportion*

$$n(\theta_A, x_A^*) = \begin{cases} 1 & \textit{if } \theta_A < x_A^* - \epsilon \\ \dfrac{1}{2} + \dfrac{x_A^* - \theta_A}{2\epsilon} & \textit{if } x_A^* - \epsilon \leq \theta_A < x_A^* + \epsilon \\ 0 & \textit{if } \theta_A > x_A^* + \epsilon \end{cases} \tag{12}$$

will withdraw in period 1. Exactly same Proposition holds for country B.

Under the monotone strategy, I can derive a property of the exchange rate as follows.

Lemma 2 (Property of the Exchange Rate). *Suppose that all the agents follow the monotonic strategy with the threshold value x_A^*. Then*

[10] Without loss of generality, I assume country A is "the first country" chosen by nature.

[11] If there is no noise in their private signals $x_{j,B}$, the observation of what happened in country A clearly does not affect their decision because they know the exact value of θ_B.

(i) $\partial e_{i1}(\theta_i, x_i^*)/\partial\theta_i \leq 0$,

(ii) $\partial e_{i2}(\theta_i, x_i^*)/\partial\theta_i \leq 0$ *if and only if*

$$S'(\theta_i, x_i^*)/S(\theta_i, x_i^*) \geq D'(\theta_i, x_i^*)/D(\theta_i, x_i^*)$$

and

(iii) $\partial e_{i2}(\theta_i, x_i^*)/\partial\theta_i \leq 0$ *if* $RX_{i2}'(\theta_i) > R'(\theta_i)$ *and* $RX_{i2}(\theta_i)/r - R(\theta_i)$ *are sufficiently large for any* θ_i,

where $S'(\theta_i, x_i^*) \equiv \partial S(\theta_i, x_i^*)/\partial\theta_i$, $D'(\theta_i, x_i^*) \equiv \partial D(\theta_i, x_i^*)/\partial\theta_i$.

Lemma 2 says that the exchange rate would devalue if and only if the economic fundamentals worsen.[12] This is reasonable because θ_i indexes "goodness" from the viewpoint of the international investors. From their viewpoint, the devaluation of the domestic currency (the increase in e_{it}) is bad since it decreases their payoffs.

So from now on, I make the following assumption.

Assumption 1 (Currency Depreciates When Economic Fundamentals Worsen).

$RX_{i2}'(\theta_i) > R'(\theta_i)$ *and* $RX_{i2}(\theta_i)/r - R(\theta_i)$ *are sufficiently large for any* θ_i.

Let θ_i^C be the threshold value of economic fundamentals in country i below which the currency crisis will occur: $D(\theta_i^C, x_i^*) = S(\theta_i^C, x_i^*)$.[13] The currency crisis happens in period 2 if and only if $\theta_i < \theta_i^C$. Recall that bank runs will happen in period 1 if and only if $n_i \geq r$. The condition $n_i \geq r$ can be reduced to $\epsilon(1-2r) + x_i^* \geq \theta_i$ by Lemma 1. Let θ_B^{BR} be the threshold value of economic

[12] Recall that currency crises will never occur if the central bank has sufficient foreign reserves to sustain the desired exchange rate. If $D(\theta_i, x_i^*) < S(\theta_i, x_i^*)$ for any θ_i, then currency crises will never occur in period 2. But we can show currency crises will occur in period 2 with some positive probability: $D(\theta_i, x_i^*) > S(\theta_i, x_i^*)$ for some θ_i. To see this, notice that $(1-w)(1-r)R(\theta_i) > Max\{0, RX_{i1} - (w + (1-w)r)\} = 0$, which ensures that $D(\theta_i, x_i^*) > S(\theta_i, x_i^*)$ when $n_i = r$. This means that if $n_i < r$ and n_i is very close to r, that bank's liquidity is threatened but not exhausted in period 1, ensuring no bank run. Currency crises will happen in period 2 in that case.

[13] θ_i^C is unique. To see this, suppose instead that there are multiple values. In that case, it must be the case that $D'(\theta_i^C, x_i^*) > S'(\theta_i^C, x_i^*)$ for at least one θ_i^C out of multiple values. But since $D(\theta_i^C, x_i^*) = S(\theta_i^C, x_i^*)$, it implies $D'(\theta_i^C, x_i^*)/D(\theta_i^C, x_i^*) > S'(\theta_i^C, x_i^*)/S(\theta_i^C, x_i^*)$, which contradicts Assumption 1. Therefore, θ_i^C must be unique.

fundamentals in country B below which bank runs will occur: $\theta_B^{BR} = \epsilon(1-2r) + x_B^*$. Clearly both the threshold value of the currency crisis (θ_B^C) and that of bank runs (θ_B^{BR}) depend on the threshold value of the monotone strategy, x_B^*. Recall also that the international investors in country B learn what has happened in country A in period 1. Thus the threshold value of the monotone strategy (x_B^*), that of the currency crisis (θ_B^C) and that of bank runs (θ_B^{BR}) might depend on what has happened in country A.

Let $x_B^*(Y_A = 1)$ and $\theta_B^C(Y_A = 1)$ be the threshold values of the monotone strategy and currency crises in country B in period 2 when bank runs or a currency crisis occur in country A in period 1, respectively. Let $x_B^*(Y_A = 0)$ and $\theta_B^C(Y_A = 0)$ be the threshold values of the monotone strategy and currency crises in country B in period 2 when no financial crises occur in country A. In my model, contagion is defined as follows.

Definition 2 (Contagion).

(i) Bank runs are contagious if $x_B^*(Y_A = 0) < x_B^*(Y_A = 1)$.

(ii) Currency crises are contagious if $\theta_B^C(Y_A = 0) < \theta_B^C(Y_A = 1)$.

Let me explain the meaning of (ii) of Definition 2 first. Consider a particular value of economic fundamentals $\tilde{\theta}_B$ such that $\theta_B^C(Y_A = 0) < \tilde{\theta}_B < \theta_B^C(Y_A = 1)$. Conditional on $\tilde{\theta}_B$, a currency crisis occurs in country B *if and only if* bank runs or a currency crisis occur in country A. As for the meaning of (i) of Definition 2, note that $x_B^*(Y_A = 0) < x_B^*(Y_A = 1)$ implies $\theta_B^{BR}(Y_A = 0) < \theta_B^{BR}(Y_A = 1)$. This defines contagious bank runs by the same reasoning as above.

In period 1 patient depositors are concerned with the payoff difference between withdrawing in period 1 and waiting until period 2. The payoff difference of interest conditional on $\theta_i, n_i, e_{i1}, e_{i2}$ can be written as follows:

$$\pi(\theta_i, n_i, e_{i1}, e_{i2}) = \begin{cases} u\left(\dfrac{(1-w)(1-\frac{n_i}{r})R(\theta_i)}{e_{i2}(1-w)(1-n_i)}\right) - u\left(\dfrac{1}{e_{i1}}\right) & \text{if } n_i \leq r \\ u(0) - u\left(\dfrac{w + (1-w)r}{e_{i1}(w + n_i(1-w))}\right) & \text{if } n_i > r \end{cases}. \quad (13)$$

As before, $n_i > r$ corresponds to the case of bank runs while $n_i \leq r$ corresponds the case of no bank runs. In the right hand side of equation (13), the first term is the payoff of waiting until period 2 while the second term is the payoff of withdrawal in period 1. If this difference is positive, it is optimal to wait until period 2.

Recall also that in period 1, the patient agents do not know the true value θ_i. But note that the patient agent j knows that θ_i must lie between $x_{j,i} - \epsilon$ and $x_{j,i} + \epsilon$ conditional on the private signal $x_{j,i}$ that he has received. So each patient agent can use this knowledge about the range of θ_A and Lemma 1 in evaluating the payoff of the withdrawal and the one of waiting. They choose the strategy which yields the higher expected utility, conditional on their own private signals. The quantity of interest to the patient agent can be written as follows:

$$\Pi(x_{j,i}) = \int_{x_{j,i}-\epsilon}^{x_{j,i}+\epsilon} \pi(\theta_i, n(\theta_i, x_i^*), e_{i1}(\theta_i, x_i^*), e_{i2}(\theta_i, x_i^*))g((\theta_i, x_i^*))d\theta_i. \quad (14)$$

If $\Pi(x_{j,i}) > 0$, it is optimal to wait until period 2. If $\Pi(x_{j,i}) < 0$, it is optimal to withdraw in period 1.

Before analyzing the monotone equilibria in detail, add the following weak assumptions to avoid this game being vacuous.

Assumption 2 (Withdraw in Period 1 if "the Worst News" Appears).

$$R(L + \epsilon) = 0. \quad (15)$$

Assumption 3 (Wait until Period 2 if "the Best News" Appears).

$$\text{(i)} \quad r(U - x) = 1 \textit{ for any } 0 \leq x \leq \epsilon \textit{ and } r(\theta_i) = \underline{r} < 1. \quad (16)$$

$$\text{(ii)} \quad R(U - \epsilon) > 1. \quad (17)$$

Assumption 2 implies that patient agents will always withdraw in period 1 if they get the worst possible news about the bank's assets returns ($x_{j,i} = L$). Conditional on $x_{j,i} = L$, the best possible return for waiting until period 2 is $R(L + \epsilon)$. On the other hand, the worst possible return of withdrawal in period 1 is $Min\{r, r/e_{i1}\}$ where r is the payoff when only banking crisis occurs and r/e_{i1} when twin crises occur. If $R(L + \epsilon) = 0$, the best possible return for waiting until period 2 conditional on $x_{j,i} = L$ is strictly smaller than the worst possible return of withdrawal in period 1. Therefore it is strictly dominant for the patient agent to withdraw in period 1 if he observes the private signal $x_{j,i} = L$. This means $\Pi(x_{j,i} = L) < 0$.

Assumption 3 implies that the patient agents will always wait until period 2 if they get the best possible news about the bank's assets returns ($x_{j,i} = U$). So far I assumed that the liquidation value of the illiquid assets is constant for any θ_i. Now I relax this assumption slightly. Part one of Assumption 3 says that if the economic fundamentals are good enough, the liquidation value is unity. That is, the risky assets are no longer illiquid. Conditional on $x_{j,i} = U$, the worst possible return for waiting until period 2 is $R(U-\epsilon)$. On the other hand, the best possible return of withdrawal in period 1 is unity. If $R(U - \epsilon) > 1$, the worst possible return for waiting until period 2 conditional on $x_{j,i} = U$ is strictly greater than the best possible return of withdrawal in period 1. Therefore, it is strictly dominant for the patient agent to wait until period 2 if he observes the private signal $x_{j,i} = U$. This means $\Pi(x_{j,i} = U) > 0$.

Now I can proceed to analyze the monotone equilibrium, which is characterized by the threshold value of the monotone strategy.

Proposition 1 (Existence of the Threshold Value x^*_A). *There exists a threshold level of signal, x^*_A, such that patient agents who receive private signals above x^*_A will wait until period 2, while those who receive private signals below x^*_A will withdraw in period 1. This means $\Pi(x_{j,A} = x^*_A) = 0$.*

Proposition 1 says that each patient agent has an incentive to wait until period 2 if and only if he observes the good signal above the threshold value.

I have considered the equilibrium strategy of the international investors who deposit in country A. Now I proceed to investigate the equilibrium strategy of those who deposit in country B. As noted above, the international investors who deposit in country B have the knowledge about what has happened in country A in period 1. Denote their knowledge by I_B. I can show that a similar proposition to Proposition 1 holds for the international investors who deposit in country B.

Proposition 2 (Existence of the Threshold Value x^*_B). *There exists a threshold level of signal conditional on I_B, $x^*_B(I_B)$, such that patient agents who receive private signals above $x^*_B(I_B)$ will wait until period 2, while those who receive private signals below $x^*_B(I_B)$ will withdraw in period 1. This means $\Pi(x_{j,B} = x^*_B(I_B)) = 0$.*

Note that the threshold value is conditional on I_B, which is the source of contagion. That is, the international investors in country B will behave conditional on what has happened in country A. Because of this, the following holds.

Proposition 3 (Contagion of Financial Crises). *Suppose financial crises occur in country* A *in period* 1. *If* $Cov(\theta_A, \theta_B) > 0$ *and private signals are noisy, financial crises spread from country* A *to country* B *in the sense that* $x^*_B(Y_A = 0) < x^*_B(Y_A = 1)$ *and* $\theta^C_B(Y_A = 0) < \theta^C_B(Y_A = 1)$.

Both the conditions that $Cov(\theta_A, \theta_B) > 0$ and that there are noises in private signals are quite critical for Proposition 3. Suppose that financial crises occur in country A in period 1. This means that the economic fundamentals of country A are expected to be quite low. If $Cov(\theta_A, \theta_B) > 0$ and private signals are noisy, financial crises in country A in period 1 would have some useful information for guessing θ_B. This would mean that the economic fundamentals in country B are likely to be low, leading international investors in country B to be more pessimistic. That is, they will update their expectation of θ_B downward. Recall that their decisions depend on $\Pi(x_{j,B})$. By updating their belief of θ_B downward, $\Pi(x_{j,B})$ shifts downward. So even when they receive moderately poor private signals, $\Pi(x_{j,B})$ tends to be negative. This means that they are more likely to withdraw their money from country B if financial crises occur in country A, leading to $x^*_B(Y_A = 0) < x^*_B(Y_A = 1)$ and $\theta^{BR}_B(Y_A = 0) < \theta^{BR}_B(Y_A = 1)$. The more (patient) investors withdraw in period 1, the more risky assets the banks have to liquidate, resulting in decreased foreign reserves in period 2. Therefore, a currency crisis is more likely to happen in country B when it occurs in country A ($\theta^C_B(Y_A = 0) < \theta^C_B(Y_A = 1)$).

Using Proposition 3, I can clarify the following three things: (1) the timing of financial crises, (2) the distinction between accidental simultaneous occurrences of financial crises and contagion due to the learning behavior, and (3) the timing of contagion. See Figure 1.[14] The vertical axis is the economic fundamentals of country A and the horizontal axis is the economic fundamentals of country B. Figure 1 depicts all possible pairs of each country's economic fundamentals. For each possible pair, my model can predict both (1) whether and when financial crises occur and (2) whether financial crises are due to contagion or not.

(1) The timing of financial crises

For example, in area 3, no crises occur either in country A or in country B. In area 8, the currency crisis occurs in country A in period 2 while no crises

[14] For a complete description of what would happen in each area of Figure 1, see Appendix A..

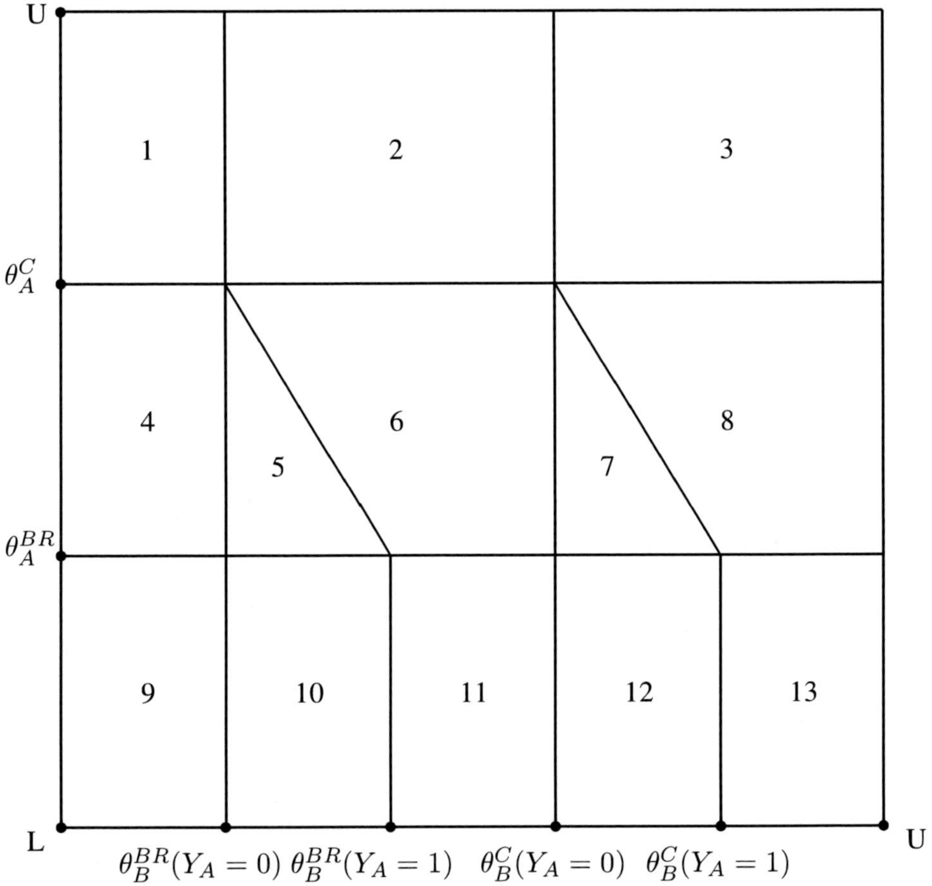

Figure 1. Timing of Financial Crises and Contagion

occur in country B. Similarly, the model can predict not only the occurrence, but also the timing of financial crises.

(2) Distinction between coincidental occurrence of crises and contagion of crises.

In area 9, twin crises occur both in country A and in country B in period 1. But conditional on the economic fundamentals in this area, twin crises will occur regardless of the actions in the other country. In this sense, there is no contagion. Put another way, this is an example of accidental simultaneous occurrence of twin crises. In areas 5, 7, 10, and 12, the financial crisis will occur in country B if and only if it occurs in country A. Thus there is contagion due to the learning behavior in these areas.

(3) Timing of contagion

In area 10, twin crises occur in country B in period 1 if and only if they occur in country A in that period. That is, the twin crises in country A in period 1 spread to country B in that period. This is "contemporaneous" contagion of twin crises.

In area 12, a currency crisis occurs in country B in period 2 if and only if twin crises in country A occur in period 1. This means that the twin crises in country A in period 1 spread to country B as the currency crisis in period 2. This is "lagged" contagion.

A different example occurs in area 5. Twin crises occur in country B first. Next, a currency crisis occurs in country A in period 2. It appears that the twin crises in country B in period 1 spread to country A as the currency crisis in period 2. That is, it appears to be lagged contagion, but the causality is actually the reverse. Recall that the international investors who deposit in country B observe how many of those who deposited in country A withdrew in period 1. In area 5, the number of depositors withdrawing money in country A in period 1 is sufficiently large that the currency crisis will occur in country A in period 2, which means many investors in country A receive signals of poor economic fundamentals. So the investors in country B become pessimistic, leading to the twin crises in period 1. I call this "forward" contagion.[15]

[15]This type of contagion captures the phenomenon that the pessimistic expectation about one country would hit another weaker country first. Look at area 5 again. In this area, the economic fundamentals in country A are relatively better than those in country B. But by observing the behavior of the international investors who deposit in country A in period 1, those who deposit in country B think that the currency crisis is very likely to happen in the next period (period 2) even though the economic fundamentals in country A are better than those in country B. So they will become pessimistic. Conditional on both their own private signals, which is likely to be low in area 5, and the pessimistic expectation, a large number of them withdraw their money in period 1, leading to twin crises in country B in period 1. That is why the weaker country suffers from financial crises in period 1 first, due to the contagion of the anticipated currency crisis in period 2.

4. Conclusion

I have constructed a micro-model of contagious twin crises (banking crises and currency crises). I have considered a situation where (1) banks in each country do not have any interbank deposits and (2) countries do not share a common lender. The model has shown that financial crises can spread even in this situation. Moreover, the model clarified (1) the timing of financial crises, (2) the distinction between accidental simultaneous occurrences of financial crises and contagion due to learning behavior, and (3) the timing of contagion. The dynamic aspect of contagion has not been investigated in detail. The model has shown that there are three types of contagion in terms of dynamics: contemporaneous contagion, lagged contagion and forward contagion. The first type is a financial crisis in one country that spreads to another country in the same period. The second type is a financial crisis in one country that spreads to another country in the next period. The third is an anticipated financial crisis in one country in the next period that spreads to another country in the period before.

A. What Happens in Each Area in Figure 1

Here is a complete description of what would happen in each area in Figure 1.

1. Twin crises occur in country B in period 1 but no crisis occurs in country A.
2. A currency crisis occurs in country B in period 2 but not in country A.
3. No crisis occurs either in country A or in country B.
4. Twin crises occur in country B in period 1 and a currency crisis occurs in country A in period 2, but it is not contagion.
5. Anticipated currency crisis in country A in period 2 leads to twin crises in country B in period 1. This is forward contagion.
6. Accidental simultaneous occurrence of currency crises in country A and country B in period 2.
7. Currency crisis in country A in period 2 leads to currency crisis in country B in period 2. This is contemporaneous contagion.

8. No crisis occurs in country B but a currency crisis occurs in country A in period 2.

9. Accidental simultaneous occurrence of twin crises in country A and country B in period 1.

10. Twin crises in country A in period 1 leads to twin crises in country B in period 1. This is contemporaneous contagion.

11. Twin crises in country A in period 1 and a currency crisis in country B in period 2 occur. This is not due to contagion.

12. Twin crises in country A in period 1 leads to a currency crisis in country B in period 2. This is lagged contagion.

13. No crisis occurs in country B, but twin crises occur in country A in period 1.

B. Proofs

B.1. Proof of Lemma 1

Notice that because of the error structure all private signals must lie between $\theta_A - \epsilon$ and $\theta_A + \epsilon$ if the true state is θ_A.

If $\theta_A < x_A^* - \epsilon$, i.e. $\theta_A + \epsilon < x_A^*$, then all private signals received by patient agents must be below the threshold value x_A^*. Under the monotone strategy, this means that all patient agents will withdraw in period 1: $n(\theta_A, x_A^*) = 1$.

If $\theta_A > x_A^* + \epsilon$, i.e. $\theta_A - \epsilon > x_A^*$, then all private signals received by patient agents must be above the threshold value x_A^*. Under the monotone strategy, this means that all patient agents will wait until period 2: $n(\theta_A, x_A^*) = 0$.

If $x_A^* - \epsilon \leq \theta_A \leq x_A^* + \epsilon$, the probability that private signals observed by patient agents are below the threshold value is

$$\frac{x_A^* - (\theta_A - \epsilon)}{2\epsilon} = \frac{1}{2} + \frac{x_A^* - \theta_A}{2\epsilon}.$$

This is exactly the expected number of patient agents who withdraw in period 1:

$$n(\theta_A, x_A^*) = \frac{1}{2} + \frac{x_A^* - \theta_A}{2\epsilon}.$$

B.2. Proof of Lemma 2

As long as $w + (1-w)n_i(\theta_i, x_i^*) < RX_{i1}$, $e_{i1}(\theta_i, x_i^*)$ remains unity for any θ_i, then $\partial e_{i1}(\theta_i, x_i^*)/\partial\theta_i = 0$. Also, as long as

$$w + (1-w)n_i(\theta_i, x_i^*) \geq w + (1-w)r \geq RX_{i1},$$

$e_{i1}(\theta_i, x_i^*)$ remains $\frac{w+(1-w)r}{RX_{i1}}$, then $\partial e_{i1}(\theta_i, x_i^*)/\partial\theta_i = 0$. If

$$w + (1-w)r \geq w + (1-w)n_i(\theta_i, x_i^*) \geq RX_{i1},$$

then

$$e_{i1}(\theta_i, x_i^*) = \frac{w + (1-w)n_i(\theta_i, x_i^*)}{RX_{i1}},$$

which is decreasing in θ_i. In sum, $\partial e_{i1}(\theta_i, x_i^*)/\partial\theta_i \leq 0$.

As long as $S(\theta_i, x_i^*) \geq D(\theta_i, x_i^*)$, $e_{i2}(\theta_i, x_i^*)$ remains unity for any θ_i, then $\partial e_{i2}(\theta_i, x_i^*)/\partial\theta_i = 0$. If $S(\theta_i, x_i^*) < D(\theta_i, x_i^*)$, then the exchange rate is $e_{i2}(\theta_i, x_i^*) = D(\theta_i, x_i^*)/S(\theta_i, x_i^*)$. In this case, it can be easily verified that $\partial e_{i2}(\theta_i, x_i^*)/\partial\theta_i \leq 0$ if and only if

$$S'(\theta_i, x_i^*)/S(\theta_i, x_i^*) \geq D'(\theta_i, x_i^*)/D(\theta_i, x_i^*).$$

Moreover,

$$S'(\theta_i, x_i^*)/S(\theta_i, x_i^*) \geq D'(\theta_i, x_i^*)/D(\theta_i, x_i^*)$$

if $S'(\theta_i, x_i^*) \geq D'(\theta_i, x_i^*)$ as long as $S(\theta_i, x_i^*) < D(\theta_i, x_i^*)$. After some algebra, the following holds.

$$S'(\theta_i, x_i^*) - D'(\theta_i, x_i^*) = \frac{1}{2\epsilon}\Big\{1 + RX_{i2}(\theta_i)/r - R(\theta_i)\Big\} + \\ \Big\{1 + n_i(\frac{1}{r} - 1)\Big\}\left\{RX'_{i2}(\theta_i) - R'(\theta_i)\right\}.$$

Since $0 \leq n_i \leq 1$ and $0 \leq r \leq 1$, $S'(\theta_i, x_i^*) > D'(\theta_i, x_i^*)$ for any θ_i if $RX'_{i2}(\theta_i) > R'(\theta_i)$ and $RX_{i2}(\theta_i)/r - R(\theta_i)$ is sufficiently large for any θ_i.

B.3. Proof of Proposition 1

Recall that in period 1, the patient agents do not know the true value θ_i. But note that the patient agent j knows that θ_i must lie between $x_{j,i} - \epsilon$ and $x_{j,i} + \epsilon$ conditional on the private signal $x_{j,i}$ that he has received. So each patient agent can use this knowledge about the range of θ_A and Lemma 1 in evaluating the payoff of the withdrawal and the one of waiting. They choose the strategy which yields the higher expected utility, conditional on their own private signals. The quantity of interest to the patient agent can be written as follows:

$$\Pi(x_{j,i}) = \int_{x_{j,i}-\epsilon}^{x_{j,i}+\epsilon} \pi(\theta_i, n(\theta_i, x_i^*), e_{i1}(\theta_i, x_i^*), e_{i2}(\theta_i, x_i^*))g((\boldsymbol{\theta_i}, \boldsymbol{x_i^*}))d\theta_i.$$

If $\Pi(x_{j,i}) > 0$, it is optimal to wait until period 2. If $\Pi(x_{j,i}) < 0$, it is optimal to withdraw in period 1. Therefore, x_A^* consists of a monotone equilibrium if the following holds.

$$\Pi(x_{j,A} = x_A^*) = 0, \tag{18}$$

$$\Pi(x_{j,A}) > 0 \text{ if } x_{j,A} > x_A^*, \tag{19}$$

$$\Pi(x_{j,A}) < 0 \text{ if } x_{j,A} < x_A^*. \tag{20}$$

From Assumption 2 and 3, $\Pi(U) > 0$ and $\Pi(L) < 0$. By continuity of $\Pi(\cdot)$, there must exist at least one value x_A^* such that $\Pi(x_{j,A} = x_A^*) = 0$ and $x_A^* \in [L, U]$. It is sufficient to show this value x_A^* satisfies (19) and (20) in order to prove this Proposition.

Note that $n(\theta_A, x_A^*) < r$, then $\epsilon(1-2r) + x_A^* < \theta_A$. Therefore, $\Pi(\cdot)$ can be written as follows:

$$\Pi(x_{j,A}) = \int_{\epsilon(1-2r)+x_A^*}^{x_{j,A}+\epsilon} \left\{ u\left(\frac{(1-w)(1-\frac{n(\theta_A, x_A^*)}{r})R(\theta_i)}{e_{A2}(\theta_A, x_A^*)(1-w)(1-n(\theta_A, \boldsymbol{x_A^*}))} \right) - u\left(\frac{1}{e_{A1}(\theta_A, x_A^*)} \right) \right\} g(\theta_A)d\theta_A$$

$$+ \int_{x_{j,A}-\epsilon}^{\epsilon(1-2r)+x_A^*} \left\{ u(0) - u\left(\frac{w + (1-w)r}{e_{A1}(\theta_A, x_A^*)(w + n(\theta_A, x_A^*)(1-w))} \right) \right\} g(\theta_A)d\theta_A.$$

Note that the second integral is always negative. Therefore $\Pi(x_{j,A} = x^*_A) = 0$ implies that the first integral must be positive. Suppose that every other patient agent follows the monotone strategy with x^*_A. For $x_{j,A} > x^*_A$, $\Pi(x_{j,A}) > 0$ because the first positive integral part increases and the second negative integral part "shrinks" (i.e. it also increases) as the private signal $x_{j,A}$ increases. Similarly, it can be shown that $\Pi(x_{j,A}) < 0$ for $x_{j,A} < x^*_A$.

B.4. Proof of Proposition 2

This can be proven similarly to Proposition 1.

B.5. Proof of Proposition 3

Financial crises in country A imply $n_A > r$. If financial crises do not occur, $n_A < r$. So I need to compare $n_A > r$ and $n_A < r$ in order to consider contagion. For simplicity, I compare $n_A = 1$ and $n_A = 0$ in this proof. The same proof applies when comparing $n_A > r$ and $n_A < r$.

First, I show

$$x^*_B(n_A = 1) > x^*_B(n_A = 0).$$

To see this, notice that $n_A = 1$ ($n_A = 0$) means that all patient depositors who deposit in country A have received private signals below (above) the threshold value x^*_A. It implies the exact value of θ_A cannot be so high (low) since private signals are positively correlated with the exact value of θ_A: $x_{j,A} = \theta_A + \epsilon_{j,A}$. It in turn means θ_B cannot be so high (low) as long as $Cov(\theta_A, \theta_B) > 0$. Thus international investors in country B will update the distribution of θ_B downward if they observe $n_A = 1$. Similarly, they will update the distribution of θ_B upward if they observe $n_A = 0$. Suppose that they observe $n_A = 1$. Recall that the threshold value x^*_B must satisfy

$$\begin{aligned}\Pi(x_{j,B} &= x^*_B(n_A = 1)) \\ &= \int_{\epsilon(1-2r)+x^*_B}^{x_{j,B}+\epsilon} \left\{ u\left(\frac{(1-w)(1-\frac{n(\theta_B, x^*_B)}{r})R(\theta_i)}{e_{B2}(\theta_B, x^*_B)(1-w)(1-n(\theta_B, x^*_B))}\right)\right. \\ &\qquad \left. - u\left(\frac{1}{e_{B1}(\theta_B, x^*_B)}\right)\right\} g(\theta_B | n_A = 1) d\theta_B\end{aligned}$$

$$+\int_{x_{j,B}-\epsilon}^{\epsilon(1-2r)+x_B^*}\left\{u\left(0\right)-u\left(\frac{w+(1-w)r}{e_{B1}(\theta_B,x_B^*)(w+n(\theta_B,x_B^*)(1-w))}\right)\right\}$$

$$\times g(\theta_B|n_A=1)d\theta_B=0.$$

The first term in the right hand side is positive which the second term in the second term is negative. Conditional on $n_A = 1$, $g(\theta_B|n_A = 1)$ will assign smaller weights on the first positive term and larger weights on the second negative term than $g(\theta_B|n_A = 0)$ will. This means that I must have $x_B^*(n_A = 1) > x_B^*(n_A = 0)$ to have

$$\Pi(x_{j,B}=x_B^*(n_A=1))=\Pi(x_{j,B}=x_B^*(n_A=0))=0,$$

which proves $x_B^*(Y_A = 1) > x_B^*(Y_A = 0)$.

Second, I show θ_B^C is strictly increasing in x_B^*. By the definition of θ_B^C,

$$D(\theta_B^C,x_B^*)=S(\theta_B^C,x_B^*). \tag{21}$$

Differentiating this, the following holds.

$$\frac{d\theta_B^C}{dx_B^*}=\frac{\partial D(\theta_B^C,x_B^*)/\partial x_B^*-\partial S(\theta_B^C,x_B^*)/\partial x_B^*}{\partial S(\theta_B^C,x_B^*)/\partial\theta_B^C-\partial D(\theta_B^C,x_B^*)/\partial\theta_B^C}. \tag{22}$$

By Assumption 1,

$$\frac{\partial S(\theta_B^C,x_B^*)/\partial\theta_B^C}{S(\theta_B^C,x_B^*)}\geq\frac{\partial D(\theta_B^C,x_B^*)/\partial\theta_B^C}{D(\theta_B^C,x_B^*)}. \tag{23}$$

Since $D(\theta_B^C, x_B^*) = S(\theta_B^C, x_B^*)$, this can be simplified as follows.

$$\frac{\partial S(\theta_B^C,x_B^*)}{\partial\theta_B^C}\geq\frac{\partial D(\theta_B^C,x_B^*)}{\partial\theta_B^C}. \tag{24}$$

From (22) and (24),

$$\frac{d\theta_B^C}{dx_B^*}>0\ \text{ if and only if }\ \frac{\partial D(\theta_B^C,x_B^*)}{\partial x_B^*}-\frac{\partial S(\theta_B^C,x_B^*)}{\partial x_B^*}>0. \tag{25}$$

After simple calculation, the following holds.

$$\frac{\partial D(\theta_B^C,x_B^*)}{\partial x_B^*}-\frac{\partial S(\theta_B^C,x_B^*)}{\partial x_B^*}=\frac{1}{2\epsilon}\left\{1-\frac{1}{r}\left(R(\theta_B^C)-RX_{B2}(\theta_B^C)\right)\right\}. \tag{26}$$

Therefore,

$$\frac{\partial D(\theta_B^C, x_B^*)}{\partial x_B^*} - \frac{\partial S(\theta_B^C, x_B^*)}{\partial x_B^*} > 0 \text{ if and only if } R(\theta_B^C) - RX_{B2}(\theta_B^C) < r. \tag{27}$$

Recall also that

$$D(\theta_B^C, x_B^*) = (1-w)(1-n(\theta_B^C, x_B^*))R(\theta_B^C), \tag{28}$$

$$S(\theta_B^C, x_B^*) = Max\Big\{0, RX_{B1} - (w + (1-w)n(\theta_B^C, x_B^*))\Big\} + (1-w)\left(1 - \frac{n(\theta_B^C, x_B^*)}{r}\right) RX_{B2}(\theta_B^C). \tag{29}$$

In (29), there are two possibilities for $Max\,\{0, RX_{B1} - (w + (1-w)n(\theta_B^C, x_B^*))\}$:

$$Max\,\{0, RX_{B1} - (w + (1-w)n(\theta_B^C, x_B^*))\} = 0 \text{ or } RX_{B1} - (w + (1-w)n(\theta_B^C, x_B^*)). \tag{30}$$

If $Max\,\{0, RX_{B1} - (w + (1-w)n(\theta_B^C, x_B^*))\} = 0$, then (21), (28) and (29) imply that $R(\theta_B^C) = RX_{B2}(\theta_B^C)$. Thus $R(\theta_B^C) - RX_{B2}(\theta_B^C) < r$ holds.

If

$$Max\,\{0, RX_{B1} - (w + (1-w)n(\theta_B^C, x_B^*))\} = RX_{B1} - (w + (1-w)n(\theta_B^C, x_B^*)),$$

the following holds.

$$R(\theta_B^C) - RX_{B2}(\theta_B^C) = \frac{RX_{B1} - (w + (1-w)n(\theta_B^C, x_B^*)}{(1-w)(1 - \frac{n(\theta_B^C, x_B^*)}{r})} < r. \tag{31}$$

The last inequality comes from the assumption $RX_{B1} < w + (1-w)r$. Therefore, $d\theta_B^C/dx_B^* > 0$ holds.

Since $x_B^*(Y_A = 1) > x_B^*(Y_A = 0)$ and $d\theta_B^C/dx_B^* > 0$, $\theta_B^C(Y_A = 1) > \theta_B^C(Y_A = 0)$ holds.

Acknowledgment

The author is deeply grateful to Steven N. Durlauf for his invaluable advice and constant encouragement. The author also thanks Yeon-Koo Che, Charles Engel, Bruce Hansen, and Bob Staiger for helpful suggestions. All possible remaining errors are mine.

References

Chang, R., and Velasco, A. (2000). Banks, debt Maturity and financial crises. *Journal of International Economics*, **51(1)**, 169–194.

Dasgupta, A. (2004). Financial contagion through capital connections: a model of the origin and spread of bank panics, *Journal of the European Economic Association*, **2**, 1049–1084.

Diamond, D. W. and Dybvig, P. H. (1983). Bank runs, deposit insurance, and liquidity. *Journal of Political Economy*, **91**, 401–419.

Eichengreen, B., Rose, A. K., and Wyplosz, C. (1996). Contagious currency crises: first tests. *Scandinavian Journal of Economics*, **98**, 463–484.

Forbes, K. J. (2004). The Asian flu and Russian virus: the international transmission of crises in firm-level data. *Journal of International Economics*, **63**, 59–92.

Frankel, J. A. and Rose, A. K. (2000). Currency crashes in emerging markets: an empirical treatment. *Journal of International Economics*, **41**, 351–366.

Furman, J., and Stiglitz, J. E. (1998). Economic crises: evidence and insights from east Asia. *Brookings Papers on Economic Activity*, 1998(2), 1–114.

Goldstein, I. and Pauzner, A. (2005). Demand deposit contracts and the probability of bank runs. *Journal of Finance*, **60**, 1293–1327.

Goldstein, M., Kaminsky, G. L., and Reinhart, C. M. (2000). *Assessing financial vulnerability: an early warning system for emerging markets*. Washington, DC: Institute for international economics.

Kaminsky, G. L. and Reinhart, C. M. (1998). Financial crises in Asia and Latin America: then and now. *American Economic Review Papers and Proceedings*, **88**, 444–448.

Krugman, P. (1999). *Balance sheets, the transfer problem, and financial crises.* In P. Isard, A. Razin, and A. K. Rose (Eds.), International finance and financial crises: essays in honor of Robert P. Flood, Jr. (pp. 31–44). Norwell: Kluwer Academic Publishers.

Masson, P. (1999a). *Contagion: monsoonal effects, spillovers, and jumps between multiple equilibria*. In P.-R. Agénor, M. Miller, D. Vines, and A. Weber (Eds.), The Asian financial crisis: causes, contagion and consequences (pp. 265–279). Cambridge: Cambridge University Press.

Masson, P. (1999b). Multiple equilibria, contagion and the emerging market crises. *IMF working paper* **99/164**.

Morris, S. and Shin, H. S. (1998). Unique equilibrium in a model of self-fulfilling currency attacks. *American Economic Review*, **88**, 587–597.

Tornell, A. (1999). Common fundamentals in the tequila and Asian crises. *NBER Working Paper* **7139**.

INDEX

#

A

B

C

J

K

L

M

N

O

P

Q

R

S

T

U

V